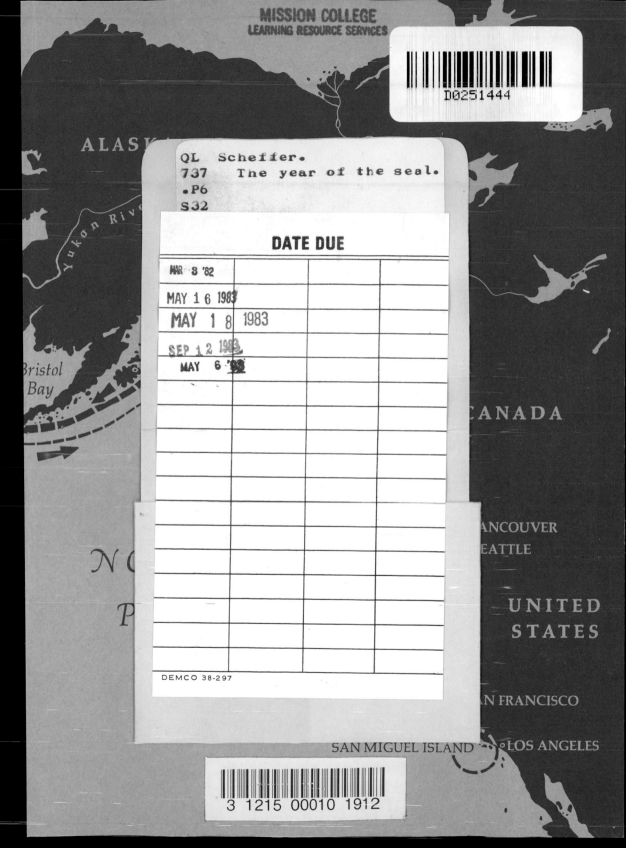

DATE DUE

MAR 3 '82			
MAY 1 6 1983			
MAY 1 8 1983			
SEP 1 2 1983			
MAY 6 '92			

DEMCO 38-297

NBCL
NJ

72

LCA

R. anuc /op/ 10⁰⁰

701273   (LF)

10/78

THE YEAR
OF THE SEAL

ALSO BY VICTOR B. SCHEFFER

The Year of the Whale

ILLUSTRATIONS BY LEONARD EVERETT FISHER

VICTOR B. SCHEFFER

THE YEAR
OF THE SEAL

New York

CHARLES SCRIBNER'S SONS

THIS BOOK PUBLISHED SIMULTANEOUSLY IN
THE UNITED STATES OF AMERICA AND IN CANADA
COPYRIGHT UNDER THE BERNE CONVENTION

B-12.70(H)

PRINTED IN THE UNITED STATES OF AMERICA

Library of Congress Catalog Card Number 74-123840

SBN 684-31116-X

In the mythos of the folk who make their living from the sea it is well known that hidden in the dark pools of the eyes of certain seals are spirits that call out to certain men. The Irish among us, and a few Scandinavians who have lived long at the edge of the sea, can hear the message best. These seals, they say, are really fisherfolk who were caught in some act displeasing to the gods and were made to live in hairy skins forever after and to wander at the will of the winds and the tides. Once in a while such a seal will save the life of a drowning sailor and will then be released from its beastly bindings. It will turn into a beautiful maid and will be the sailor's wife, but there will be no off-spring from the union, and the old women in the village will know the reason why. Always dark-brown of eye and soft of body these beautiful creatures are, and they lie awake in bed when the full moon streams through the window.

And their feet are a bit colder than the feet of ordinary women.

PREFACE

Like all other writers on zoology I have set myself an impossible task: to interpret for human understanding the thoughts and motivations, the movements and life processes, of a nonhuman animal, in this case the Alaska fur seal. Though the life of a seal is apparently simple, rude, instinctive, and devoid of the luxury of choice, it will forever hold its final secrets and will forever challenge the zoologist. He will never be able to *know* the seal or truly to sympathize with it, even though at moments he may look upon a little seal as simply a small person wrapped in fur and endowed prematurely with mustaches. Seal and man are doomed forever to travel apart in their strange and separate ways.

A year in the life of a seal is an ordinary year; repetitive, ritualistic, undramatic. In summer the female gives birth on land, copulates, nurses her pup; in the fall she goes to sea for many months, returning to land in summer, again to give birth and copulate. How does a writer work this stuff into a story containing the central message that humans are richer for sharing a world with seals? My own solution has been to bring humans into the story often and to translate as best I can the excitement I have felt in learning about seals and in listening to others telling what they have learned.

Most of the men in my story are wildlife-research biologists. They are composites of real men I have known and respected, men driven by the question *why*? At times such men leave their homes for months on end, endure seasickness, and work in cold, bloody, filthy surroundings. Each one takes his reward in pride of accomplishment.

Each is content to watch the cairn of scientific truth rise a little higher each year. The pebble each man puts in place is his piece of immortality.

Some of the men who enter the narrative are Pribilof natives. Their ancestors were full-blooded Aleuts who were pressed into labor by Russian fur-seekers in the eighteenth century and were translocated to the barren Pribilof Islands. Their descendants became, in 1867, wards of the United States Government. Today, many of the Pribilof natives are indistinguishable in physical features and in habits from Americans of European stock, and all of the natives are American citizens in the full sense of the word. They are the stewards of the great Alaska fur-seal herd.

Whether I write of seals or of men, my narrative is fiction based on fact. The life of the seals is described from a seal point of view; the accounts of the biologists' activities, the biology of seals, commercial sealing, and conservation reflect a human point of view. Because people often look at the peculiar form of a seal and ask, "Where did seals come from?", I have given a résumé of theories of their origin (Appendix, pages 181–187). This résumé is a prehistory beginning thirty million years or more before the opening of the present story. The sources of quotations, documentation of real events, and explanations of the origins of fictional people and ships are given in the Reference Notes (pages 189–192). To avoid interrupting the text with reference numbers, the notes are identified by the number of the page and the line or lines to which they refer. In addition, I have provided a bibliography, consisting of seven important accounts in the literature of seals and sealing.

VICTOR B. SCHEFFER

CONTENTS

xi

THE YEAR
OF THE SEAL

PROLOGUE:

APPROACHING THE YEAR OF THE SEAL

This is the great deep-sea song that all the St. Paul seals sing when they are heading back to their beaches in the summer. It is a sort of very sad seal National Anthem.

I met my mates in the morning (and oh, but I am old!)
Where roaring on the ledges the summer ground-swell rolled;
I heard them lift the chorus that drowned the breakers' song—
The Beaches of Lukannon—two million voices strong!

The song of pleasant stations beside the salt lagoons,
The song of blowing squadrons that shuffled down the dunes,
The song of midnight dances that churned the sea to flame—
The Beaches of Lukannon—before the sealers came!

RUDYARD KIPLING, "The White Seal"

3

+ +
+ + +

THE beaches of Lukannon are still there today, though the name is now spelled Lukanin, and the seals still come back each year in summer. The men who hunted them down with guns are long departed from this earth, and their places have been taken by new men who have arranged a sort of truce with the seals.

In Kipling's story of seals, men also have a part. My story tells of a Golden Seal and of men who watch her and care for her in all months of the year. Some of them probe deeply into her life to study the peculiar adaptations of body form and function that enable this beautiful animal to move freely between land and sea, a creature of two worlds and a mistress of both.

Of the group of animals now known as the Pinnipedia—or seals, sea lions, and walruses—the great Swedish naturalist Carolus Linnaeus wrote two hundred years ago:

"This is a dirty, curious, quarrelsome tribe, easily tamed, and polygamous; flesh succulent and tender; fat and skin useful. They inhabit and swim under water and crawl on land with difficulty because of their retracted fore-feet and united hind-feet; feed on fish and marine productions, and swallow stones to prevent hunger, by distending the stomach."

The word *pinnipedia* is Latin for "fin-footed." It could well be applied to all marine mammals, for all of them have at least one pair of limbs flattened for swimming or steering. In formal zoology, though, it is applied only to seals.

PROLOGUE

Our ancestors gave many names to the seal-kind. They called them sea-dogs, sea-cats, sea-wolves, sea-bears, and sea-lions. They called a baby seal a pup and a baby walrus a calf. "Walrus" comes from the Norwegian *hvalros*—whale-horse. Now we are stuck with their terminology. Long ago I stopped worrying about vernacular names. "Gopher" means turtle in Florida, ground-squirrel in Minnesota, and pocket-gopher in Oregon; I accept the dialect.

Of the thirty-three species of seals that live in the salt and fresh waters of the world, I have chosen to write about one, the Alaska fur seal *(Callorhinus ursinus)*, because it is outstanding. It assembles at the breeding season in numbers so great that a man crouching on a cliff-top above a rookery can count tens of thousands. Nowhere else in the world, I think, could he see so many mammals from one vantage point, unless perhaps at the entrance to Carlsbad Caverns, New Mexico, where the bats in flight come pouring forth at dusk to feed.

Of all the pinnipeds, the Alaska seal spends the greatest part of its yearly cycle remote from land or ice. For seven or eight months in winter and spring it feeds and sleeps on the open Pacific. Its flippers are never dry in winter. The only solid thing they touch is the sleek body to which they are bound, and which they groom and scrub in endless play of motion. During this pelagic, or oceanic, phase of its year the Alaska seal travels the longest migratory path of any pinniped, up to six thousand miles from start to return.

Of all the pinnipeds, and perhaps of all the mammals of the world, the Alaska seal shows the greatest difference in body size between sexes. The average grown male, or bull, weighs four and one-half times as much as the female, or cow,—that is, about 450 pounds as against 100. This curious difference is related to the strong territorial instinct of seals, and to polygamy, both of which are discussed later.

For still another reason I have chosen the Alaska seal as the central figure of this narrative. Because its kind has never lived in European waters, the classical writers of the Old World have not belabored its natural history.

The first European, in fact, to see a fur seal was the German naturalist Georg Wilhelm Steller (1709-1746), on the voyage of discovery of mainland Alaska. At shimmering twilight on August 10, 1741, south of the island now known as Kodiak, he watched a "sea ape" playing about the ship. He did not then or later recognize it as a seal. In the next summer, while shipwrecked on Bering Island, he watched in amazement as the fur seals returned to the beaches to breed. Through the publication of his "De Bestiis Marinis" in 1751, the fur seal became known to science.

Finally, a special glamour surrounds the Alaska seal because wealthy women have wanted to wear its brown coat, and men have killed one another to obtain the coats, and politicians have lied in order to profit from the skinning of the seals while statesmen and zoologists—rare associates indeed—have joined in public testimony to

6

save the seals from extermination. Today, the seal industry brings a revenue of five million dollars a year. To those who are impressed by such figures, this will be an impressive figure. Meanwhile, the dripping seals arrive on land in summer and disappear in the sea fogs of autumn. With the great mystery and wonder of their animal lives I am deeply concerned; for the price on their heads I care little.

The principal character in my story is called the Golden Seal, for down the sides of her breast her jacket shines with a yellowish hue, a color variation seen in one of a thousand individuals. She was marked this way from her first summer, when she molted her black puppy hair and assumed the bright coat of the young adult. When my story begins, she is exactly four years old, and, in fact, all her companions are at, or near, their birthday anniversaries, since all fur seals are born in midsummer. There is a curious reason for this, which is explained later.

The part of the story that takes place on land is chiefly set on St. Paul Island, most northerly of the Pribilof Islands (also called the Fur Seal Islands) in Bering Sea off the coast of Alaska. Much of the action occurs on Tolstoi rookery. The lower edge of this rookery follows the curve of the sea for a thousand yards. The rookery proper is above, a sandy flat strewn with rocks. Still higher, the land rises sharply to a green, grassy ridge rarely visited by seals.

How Tolstoi got its name is lost in the prehistory of St. Paul Island. The Russians landed here in 1786 (or was it 1787?) and began at once to exploit the riches of seal and sea-otter skins, and of walrus ivory. Now the otters and the walruses are gone, and the story of the name is gone. Perhaps patron Tolstoi was a noble ancestor of writer Leo Nikolaevich; perhaps he was only a boat-steerer under Captain-Commander Gerasim Pribilof; or perhaps the name was derived from the Russian *tol'stoi* (thick), in reference to the cliffs. The word "rookery" originated long ago as the name for a noisy, dirty gathering place of birds, such as European rooks. As applied to a seal beach now, it means a common where females give birth and nurse their pups, and where, while they are captives (so to speak) of their young, they are bred by the bulls. A seal rookery in summer is a country forbidden to adolescent seals and cripples, and to all other members of seal society unable or unwilling to breed.

I have chosen the month of July as the starting point of the year of the seal, since most seals are born in that month. It is fitting that a biography should start on a note of renewal and promise for the species.

JULY

A thin cry like the bleat of a newborn lamb is lifted by the wind and carried along the shore. It speaks of fright, and of a strange world, and of cold air, and of the bitter spray that rises from breaking waves. It speaks of beastly forms moving around and above the source of the cry, their shapes all dark and dimly seen.

In a pool of black mud, a black fur-seal pup struggles to free himself from a gauzy membrane—the amniotic sac in which he is being delivered from the womb of his mother. His mother, the Golden Seal, arches her back and pushes her nose against his body. In the dim past of her race, a mother-animal, somewhere and sometime in a cave, would seize her offspring, free it from the birth sac, and lick it clean. But few of these maternal duties does the Golden Seal now perform; she and her kind are gone too long from the cave. Before she dies she will give birth to five more pups and will miscarry one. Each will be a replicate of the one before it, and in the process of each birth she will offer only the simplest of care, an abbreviated ritual of mother love. Now she nuzzles her baby and sucks in deeply the odor of his wet, steaming body. She learns to identify this one creation among thousands like him, so that soon, when she begins her summer-long schedule of giving milk, she will be able to find her own pup at each nursing time in a mob of thirsty little strangers.

The pup staggers wildly through the filth of the rookery, dragging the placenta on its short umbilical cord. Instinctively, he pushes toward the warmest part of mother's body, the left side of her belly where she has lain toward the sun. He shakes convulsively; he rolls his dark eyes; he lifts his muzzle to the sky and gives a cry that pierces the wind.

Above the full chorus of a thousand voices, young and old, it threads its way along the corridors of gray volcanic boulders standing erect and polished by the shoulders of generations of seals. It floats across an open tundra where yellow arctic poppies dance on the summer days. It carries at last, this thin cry, to the ears of a great bull seal who lies with unseeing eyes on a slab of rock above Tolstoi rookery. He is dying.

Here he crawled in June, out of the Bering Sea of Alaska, up the slanting shore of St. Paul Island, across green sands manured by the seals of the previous year, onto the slab of rock, here at last to lie without food or drink for a month. Age and illness and a thousand little deaths have done him in. The urge to return in spring and to challenge his fellow males for a beachhead has brought him once again to the place where he was born twenty-four years ago. In breaching the surf for a landing he was attacked by a younger bull, and he suffered a deep wound from ear to throat. In the days of his prime the red gash would have healed, but now the tissues will not close. Paralyzed, quiet, staring toward the sea—his other home —he hears a last sound, the testimony of a new life.

In early July the pupping season on Tolstoi is at peak. Seals are born at the rate of one every two minutes, day and night. A vast continuous undertone, like the roar of a crowd in a sports arena, or a distant waterfall, is pierced briefly by the cries of individual pups and by the raging of white gulls fighting for bits of rookery debris. Five hundred bulls of breeding age, the "harem" bulls, are stationed on individual territories. Ten thousand breeding females are sprawled on the ground beside them, resting or nursing; two thousand females with newborn young are feeding in Bering Sea, preparing to return to their pups on the rookery; and ten thousand females heavy with unborn young are still moving north to Tolstoi, soon to rest their bodies on land after many months at sea.

On the morning of the third of July, the Golden Seal gently seizes her pup by the scruff of his neck and drags him up the slope of Tolstoi out of the mud to a sandy, well-drained clearing. She would carry him farther, to the lee of a rock, but the harem bull sees the movement from the corner of his eye and comes rolling toward her with ponderous gait and a menacing "Chunk! chunk! chunk!" from his open jaws.

Here on the sand the mother rests, while the birth blood dries on her flanks and the rich gold of her breast fur glows in the dawning light. The color blends with the gold of the crinkly lichens that decorate the rock face beyond her.

The pup has found a black nipple the size of a man's little-finger tip—one of four on her belly—and has pulled it for the first time from its crypt in the fur. He has suckled and is replete. He sleeps heavily, snoring, and the mother sleeps. She is very tired, for she is a small seal,—she weighs only 50 pounds—and she has brought to light a 10-pound baby. She twitches in a dream. She "swims" in jerky motions of her naked hands. Her nostrils flare at long intervals to breathe. She is not yet wholly a creature of the land but is locked-in on the rhythm of the sea.

Her black whiskers twitch as the little kelp flies crawl upon them. These fuzzy animalcules, discouraged by the Bering chill, are seldom known to fly; they carry out their appointed tasks at a crawl. They mate in slow motion, wearing fur coats, or so the St. Paul natives say; they call them the "fur-bearing flies."

The days go by, and on the seventh of July the Golden Seal comes suddenly in heat. Her womb is shaped like a V, with two horns that function in alternate years. The newly emptied horn, which was of monstrous size on the first of July, is shrinking rapidly to the size of a lemon and is draining cleanly. In the other horn, no thicker than a pencil, a ripe egg is moving down from the ovary. Chemical messengers in her blood tell the Golden Seal that now is her appointed time.

Mother and pup have been lying at the edge of a

territory guarded by a twelve-year-old, 440-pound bull. He outweighs her more than eight to one. This is only his third year as a harem bull, but it is also his last. The competition on Tolstoi is so fierce, and the turnover among breeding males is so rapid, that next summer he will find his station preempted by a newcomer, a bull no stronger but more aggressive.

Now the bull circles his territory, clambering over rocks and trampling brutally on the flippers of any seals that happen to be in his way. He smells the nose of each female, one by one, in a curious ritual that brings a bouquet of white whiskers sharply to the front of his snout. He is searching for a female in heat, which will be indicated by the yeasty smell of her breath. In the act of nosing, he shows no affection, but rather suspicion bordering on hostility.

When he reaches the upper rim of his territory he sees that the Golden Seal has deserted her pup for the first time in nearly a week and is standing a few yards from the sleeping baby. He advances, touches her nose, sniffs, and gives a low snort of excitement. She responds with a hiss. Both call-notes are part of a threat pattern; they seem out of place as overture to the love play about to begin. The bull circles awkwardly and tries to smell her hindquarters, but she turns quickly and bites his throat. The nip has no effect through the protective armor of hair, fur, skin, and blubber.

Now the pair circle and joust in a clumsy dance on the rotting debris of Tolstoi beach. They rub noses repeatedly. Their whiskers interlock. She bites his neck and then his lower jaw. He roars and hisses and chuckles. She finally pauses, boosts her back, and allows him to smell her attractive rear, swollen and flaring a brilliant pink. He mounts, dog fashion, and impregnates her in a six-minute act. So great is the difference in weight between the pair that her head is barely visible under his chest, and her dark eyes bulge.

A rank, musky, wet-dog odor rises from his sweat glands. Oh, but he stinks! "Web-footed Seals forsake the stormy swell, and sleep in herds, exhaling nauseous smell . . ." wrote Homer.

The bull saunters away and takes up patrol where he left off. Today he will search out and mate with three other females. The Golden Seal lies quietly until she hears the cry of her hungry pup. She returns to his side and nurses him. Later she will try again to attract the bull, but he will only pause briefly to smell her rear before he moves along.

✦✦✦

NORTH of the hill of Tolstoi lies a soft, open plain, above which the rounded remains of old volcanoes rise to the sky. The plain recalls Wyoming in spring, but here there is no tree or shrub. On the hilltop a willow spreads its branches, covered with catkins, in a mat 10 feet across, but the whole plant is only as high as a man's ankle. Straight away, the twin breasts of Polovina curve against the skyline. Polovina is a warm, comfortable hill, a lovely hill. Now and again the sun breaks through the low clouds and traces the hill's contours in a drifting spotlight of greeny gold.

On the ridge of Tolstoi a man appears. He is a biologist, and he carries a fishpole. He is in his middle fifties, roughly built, with a face reddened by ocean winds. The straps of a yellow sou'wester are tied beneath his chin; a raincoat hangs to his knees, while hip-length boots complete the uniform of the day. The raincoat is a sorry thing, all splotched with blood, bile, and laboratory chemicals. Its hem has been torn by the teeth of angry seals.

Twenty-five years ago, the biologist was graduated from a western university with the degree of Master of Science in Wildlife Management. He was one of a small band in the whole United States with that degree, for his specialty was new and the textbooks in his field were few. He studied the classic life sciences, botany and zoology, and then he learned to read a contour map, to mount bird and mammal skins for study, to perform autopsies on animals, to press plants for herbarium use, to photograph things out-of-doors and through the microscope, to identify the sticky remains of food in the stomachs of wild animals, and to analyze the figures derived from endless counts and measurements. He learned, finally, how to write a lucid report of investigations in the field. Later, when he left school, he tackled the real job of managing wildlife populations and wildlife environments. He learned tricks that were not in the book, such as how to get a truck wheel out of freezing gumbo mud in the dark of night, how to build a campfire in the rain, and how to skin a skunk without losing friends. And at some invisible turning in his path, a feeling for the beauty of wilderness came to dwell forever in his soul.

He now descends through the wet grass of Tolstoi to the edge of the rookery. Moving slowly, so as not to frighten the seals, he climbs a short ladder that puts him on a catwalk, a wooden structure 500 feet long. It is a trail 6 feet above the rookery where a man can walk above the heads of the seals and be well out of reach of their sharp teeth. He stops. He bends down with the fishpole, line and hook, and snags the lifeless body of a pup wedged between two rocks. He lifts the malodorous thing, numbers it with a tag, and places it in a burlap bag, then moves along the walkway. Every second day in July he has followed the same routine, collecting the bodies of pups that died since his last inspection of the route. By ten o'clock he has gathered fourteen specimens. In his laboratory in St. Paul village he dons rubber gloves and, with a scalpel, examines the little bodies post mortem.

The biologist realizes that men can seldom soften the impact of natural mortality upon a wild creature, that one-shot treatments are not often effective. The short-term benefit turns out to be the long-term liability. Doctors of men and doctors of wildlife agree that a decent, uncrowded environment is the best guarantee of health and long life. They know that the quickest way to improve body condition among men and other animals is to improve the surroundings in which they feed, and breed, and rear their young.

Because the critical factor in life is often the food supply—the basic energy input wildlife biologists look first at the possibilities of increasing food. The best method of doing this is to kill a planned percentage of the population. Though ethics prevents the doctor of men from using this straightforward tool, the biologist may do so to raise quality, at the expense of quantity, of life. Actually, in a wildlife population such as the Alaska seal herd, which is cropped by the deliberate killing of tens of thousands of its members, the numbers that man can withdraw year after year for his own use are greatest when the level of the population stands at only half its primitive or potential size. The final goal of fur-seal management is "maximum sustainable yield." Whether the yield be skins, or meat, or other economic goods is of secondary importance.

In performing autopsies on the Tolstoi pups, the biologist's first purpose is to record the causes of death at the present level of seal-herd size. He is asking, in effect, Will the causes shift in importance as the population changes in the future—as it becomes more, or less, crowded? He is constantly aware of the need to monitor the situation of the moment, to feel its pulse, so that he can make comparisons, draw conclusions, and eventually make predictions. To the extent that he becomes clairvoyant will he become a useful member of his profession.

In the second place, he wants to understand the causes of death so that he can recommend preventive measures. If, for example, many pups show symptoms of ruptured internal organs, he will suspect that the pups have difficulty in escaping the rushes of the older seals, and he will recommend that workmen push boulders onto the flat rookery so that the pups can hide in their shelter.

At the end of the morning, he tallies the percentage causes of death by malnutrition, hookworm anemia, injuries, infections, and other causes, including birth misfortunes. The item "malnutrition" is a catch-all word to include the mysterious factors that cause a pup to lose weight and to wander about the rookery, crying piteously, shivering, and finally passing into its last sleep. Was its mother killed? Or did she have no milk for her baby? Or did the pup lose appetite through some disease? Who can say? Little starvelings are a common sight on Tolstoi, where the natives call them "orphans."

When evening falls, the biologist sits in his room and relaxes with his favorite books, the chronicles of Arctic and Antarctic adventure. His cabin is muffled in mist. Faintly through the curtains come the polytones of the island: the voices of the seals on the Reef, the distant barking of a fox, the sleepy calls of the night birds. Time dissolves in a blur. He is standing on the southern ice in 1912 beside the frozen body of Robert Falcon Scott. He is reading the last message of that gallant man to his wife: "Make the boy interested in natural history if you can; it is better than games; they encourage it at some schools."

+ + +

THE Golden Seal is restless this afternoon. She is ready to abandon her pup for a few days and return to the sea. Her body tissues cry for moisture. Her fur is dirty and smelly. She has given up a gallon of milk, a rich milk with a fat content of more than 40 percent. She looks down at the small dark thing that came from her loins, and she looks away toward the sea where it breaks wetly on the rocks.

Suddenly she starts in alarm. Overhead the whine of an airplane grows above the roar of the surf. It is a new and dangerous sound. A twin-engined craft settles to the airstrip north of Polovina, dropping after a flight of three hours from Anchorage.

As the plane glides in from the sea above the rookeries of the Reef, the passengers look down and see black-iron filings held on a brown plate by a magnet underneath. "Why, they're *seals—millions* of them!"

The visitors are caught in the excitement of the sharp break between the mainland forests and this bare oceanic island. They step stiffly from the plane and soon are intoxicated. They are intoxicated by waves of color—the ultraviolet of sky reflected from tundra flowers: blue lupine, red and purple fernleaf, purple primrose, pale blue for-get-me-not, indigo monkshood, pink moss campion, and the hues of other plants that burst in a riot of bloom to insure their fruiting while the brief summer holds.

In July, too, the sweet voices of the land birds rise upward and everywhere—the calls of the longspur, snow bunting, sandpiper, and rosy finch. The rare, bubbling song of a wren comes faintly from cliffs along the sea. The calls thread back and forth from dawn to dark. They hold deep meaning to the frail creatures that give them voice, and they offer a spirit-welcome to the tourist visitors from Anchorage. The colors and sounds of St. Paul Island all tell of a detached little world that has lived through centuries of time without the clever help of man and his institutions and devices—the kind of world that will forever pull at heartstrings and cry, "Turn back, turn back . . . this is the mother source!"

The Golden Seal has made up her mind to leave the nursery. Down she goes, clambering over rocks and drift-wood and the bodies of her sisters, dodging their snap-ping teeth as best she can. Some of the seals are dry and dirty-brown like herself; some are wet and silvery clean. These have just returned from deep-sea fishing trips like the one upon which she is about to embark. She catches a flipper in a crevice and, as she struggles to free herself, drops of yellow milk spurt from a teat. At last she hits the tidal zone. Eagerly starting to swim with her flippers on the sandy beach itself, she heads for a breaking comber, shoots beneath it, and rises 30 yards beyond, leaving a muddy trail in the green waters of Bering Sea.

Meanwhile, the tourists from Anchorage are rattling along in trucks over the red pumice road to the village and to the dormitory where they will spend the night. During the night they lie awake for a while, restless in the absence of city noise, but at last they sleep profoundly, lulled by the wind crooning at the corners of the frame building. After a breakfast of thick flapjacks, thick bacon, and thick coffee, they visit Tolstoi in the company of a native guide, a boy eighteen years of age who tells them of the pattern of life of the seals, their comings and go-ings, and the things yet mysterious about their ways. He knows the chronicle well, for he was born in St. Paul village and left it only once—to attend high school at Sitka. He is known as the Two-Story Kid, for at six feet one he towers above the heads of the other Pribilof Islanders.

"Are the fur seals *mean?*" asks the lady from Cleveland. "What *good* are they?" And, finally, "How many times can you skin them?" The Kid swallows and asks himself, How did I get into this racket? He answers to the best of his ability.

A camera buff from Seattle, with more nerve than sense, slips away from the group at Observation Point and penetrates the harem of the Golden Seal. He does not realize his danger; he could be struck and torn by the bull. He focuses on a mother seal in labor and shoots 50 feet of film. The bull grows vaguely aware of an intruder but does not see or smell him. His brute mind translates the uneasy feeling as a threat, or sexual competition. He blindly seizes the nearest cow by the throat and hurls her 15 feet through the air. She circles high and lands heavily on the rocks while a red fountain starts from her throat; he had cut an artery. She sinks, uncomprehending, and in four minutes is dead. The photographer misses the tragic byplay. He returns elated with his pictures.

Toward the middle or end of July—the time varies from year to year with the weather—the annual "breakup" of harem life on Tolstoi begins. The family structures loosen. The bulls grow quieter; they retreat to the sea when a man approaches. On Tolstoi today there is no sign that the breakup is imminent, though the weather may change tomorrow.

The Golden Seal's pup has been sleeping without break since she left him yesterday. Now he drowsily wakens and looks around, though he is not alarmed by his mother's absence. At this stage in life he is only concerned about milk, and at the moment he is not hungry. His little belly bulges like a melon. He tries to scratch an itchy spot where his navel is healing; he cannot quite reach it with his flipper, so he mounts a rough pumice boulder and rides it blissfully back and forth.

A dozen yards away, something strange is happening. A half-sister of his mother is giving birth to a white seal.

The normal pup is glossy black with only a trace of

white in the armpits. The eyes are as black as those of an oriental doll, though when the full sun strikes them at a certain angle they give back sparks of deep brown.

The fur of the strange pup is creamy yellow and sopping wet; when it dries it will turn cotton white. Its flippers and eyes are pure pink. It blinks and squints and turns its head toward the dark rocks as though irritated by the daylight. The mother reacts toward the little freak exactly as she would toward a normal pup, with no more and no less attention to it. Only the biologist will know, when he peers down from the walkway tomorrow and sees this pup, that it represents one in a hundred thousand born. The slim probability of an albino birth is well established, since a white seal among black ones can be spotted from a great distance and biologists have been watching the rookeries of the Pribilof Islands for a long time.

✦✦✦

THE fur-seal laboratory on St. Paul Island is a building of solid masonry that lies like a sphinx with its rump in a great dune of volcanic ash. Between its paws it holds a little fancy yard, or pavement, of smooth black boulders which were lugged up from the beach by a biologist homesick for his patio in faraway California. On the pavement there sits a huge iron container like the cannibal pot of the cartoons, a relic of a day when sealmeat-and-corn-meal pudding was cooked over driftwood fires, to be scattered later on the tundra for the foxes.

This morning at ten o'clock a biologist stomps across the pavement, shaking sand from his boots and touching the rusty pot with a gloved hand in passing. It is the hour of the coffee break, when a half-dozen biologists and other workmen are wont to gather in the laboratory for talk and warmth. The newcomer is the oldest of the lot, ready to retire after thirty years of government service. Long ago he had been sent to the Pribilofs as a green biologist with a Ph.D. diploma and instructions to estimate the age-and-sex composition of the fur-seal millions. Little did he know that ten years would pass before the first reliable figures would be in his hands!

Now he can explain that the mystery of the fur-seal population started in the Russian regime and was unresolved through many long years of American ownership. It stemmed in part from a very human fault: the sealers were unwilling to kill female animals, the sacred cows. And, lacking data on the main element in the herd—the breeding females—the fur-seal managers could not take a proper census. They could only assume that all adult females are productive.

Even a devoted civil servant in the Washington Office, directing the affairs of the seal herd by telegraph, should have known that nature is imperfect—that seals, like men and women, suffer reproductive failures for reasons anatomical, physiological, or psychological. But the

Washington office continued to grind out annual reports of the seal industry, supported by neat rows of figures showing the numbers of seals born and dying during the year. At a lively pregnancy rate of 100 percent the herd grew on paper until it contained exactly 3,613,653 seals. On paper, the average harem bull was the putative father of 94.55 pups! These figures were clearly three times larger than life and, shortly after they were published, the Washington office lost faith in its method of computation.

The old biologist speaks of his frustration in those early years when no one was allowed to kill a female seal. He recalls the thrill of handling a small fetus which came to him by accident. A fur seal had been drowned in a fish net off the Oregon coast, on the bottom in 240 feet of water. The carcass was delivered to his laboratory in Seattle, and he carefully removed a perfect fetus only 13 ounces in weight. Its ears were flat like a puppy dog's, and on its front flippers were miniature claws—vestigial structures that would have disappeared before birth. Its body surface was like the skin of a peach.

For several years around 1950, the biologists used to go to Sitka each winter to study the pregnancy rate in seals taken by the Tlingit Indians. As "aborigines" the natives had the right—and still do have the right—to kill seals by primitive methods in traditional hunting waters. It seems odd that the natives could kill the female seals while the men responsible for the welfare of the herd could not.

Eventually, the Washington office was fully converted to the value of seal research, even if it meant the loss of seals that otherwise would have yielded up their skins to the market. The research program grew rapidly, reaching a peak in a summer when more than 47,000 females were killed in a combined effort to prune the population and to provide research data. The pregnancy rate of the Pribilof seals turned out to be 60 percent, not 100.

AS the days dwindle to the end of July the Golden Seal is far at sea on her third fishing trip. If by magic an unseen recorder could have been scribing the life of this little mother with a first-born young, the record would read as follows:

On July the first, she hauled out on the beach of Tolstoi. On the second, she gave birth to a male pup, head first, at the end of five minutes' labor. On the seventh, she came in heat and was impregnated for the second time in her life, in the resting horn of the womb. On the eighth, she went to sea to recover strength, leaving the pup asleep on the rocks. On the fifteenth, she returned to a ravenous youngster and nursed him often over a period of two days. She did not know that her mate had left the rookery, never to return, or that her harem was now ruled by another bull. On the seventeenth, she went to sea on her second fishing trip. On the twenty-sixth, she returned to Tolstoi. On the twenty-eighth, she went to sea for the third time and is now out there in the fog.

She will repeat the nursing cycles with great regularity. Her schedule is known from field observations and from studies of seal teeth. As long as any seal lives, it carries a record of its suckling days in light-and-dark bands of ivory in the roots of the teeth. If the biologist cuts a wafer-thin section of the root and holds it against a light, he can read the record.

AUGUST

The pup of the Golden Seal is roused from sleep at four in the morning by the clatter of a wooden club against the rocks at the edge of Tolstoi. A man rises in the murky light, cursing the slippery footing as he recovers his weapon and follows the man ahead of him toward the beach. Four natives are moving along in single file; they are out for a kill.

The summer day dawns in a dismal shroud of fog, and the temperature hovers at 40 degrees. A blanket of mist throws back the sounds of the seals and the men. The rocks drip, and the grasses drip, and the noses of the men drip. The fine hairy leaves of the lupine are jeweled with dew, magnified in the growing light. All around the pup, other seals in the rookery crane their necks to see the source of the clatter, but the men are gone in the fog, crouching low as they dodge among the rocks and the grassy hummocks. A bull shakes his head in annoyance; showers of muddy droplets fly from his mane. This morning, on the first of August, the little pup is hearing the sounds of a sealing kill, the final kill of the summer season.

The men reach the wide sandy beach that limits the rookery on the north, where the bachelors and the crippled and the idle seals are sleeping. From the far end of the beach other groups of running men appear in ghostly outline—and still others. Suddenly, they close ranks in a pincers' play between the seals and the water's edge. Rising to full height, they shout, "Hai! hai!" The seals throw themselves on the sand and on one another in queer postures of panic, while their flippers pound like rain. A few of them dodge between the drivers to gain the safety of the sea; the rest turn their heads inland. Their bodies steam in the morning chill; the rims of their eyes roll whitely; their frightened voices cry, "Aargh! aargh!" The smells of wet bodies, and crushed seaweed underfoot, and excrement quickly spent add a sharp dimension to the scene. The men shout "Hai! hai!" again and poke the seals gently with their clubs. One driver has brought a 5-gallon can that he drums with a seal bone found on the beach. When a few seals suddenly take the lead and move inland, toward the tundra plateau, the others stampede in the same direction.

The slapping vibration of four hundred bodies against the earth carries to the little pup, but by now he has fallen back into sleep. Nervous mothers on the rookery pick their way down to the sea. The gray sky lifts.

In the mass of seals moving across the tundra like a lava flow, the agile ones—the two-, three-, and four-year-olds—are cantering far ahead, leaving trails of darker green through the dew. The bulls are huffing and puffing and falling behind, along with a few orphan pups that were caught up in the drive because they had forsaken the nursery for the comfort of warmth among the bodies of the sleeping bachelors.

32

AUGUST

Along toward five o'clock the seals on Tolstoi can clearly see in the new light the panorama below: the white curve of the breaking sea, the empty hauling ground crisscrossed with tracks, the killing field beyond, now dotted with the black figures of men and seals, and the gray-green slopes of the distant hills.

The killing starts. The clubbers move in first. With clubs like long baseball bats they tease out from the roundup a score of animals (a pod) and with a skill developed through years of practice select the ones of prime commercial value. These they knock down with one enthusiastic stroke on the top of the head. They drag each limp, unconscious body into a work-line, shouting "One! two! a-three!" ... and so on till they fill a tally line of ten. A sticker gives the *coup de grâce* with a steel knife; the heart-blood burbles on the grass. The slitter makes a few deft cuts around the black flippers; white furrows of blubber-fat show quickly in the trail of his blade. Finally, three strippers jerk the pelt loose in a concerted lunge and peel it off like a great warm glove. They throw it on the ground to cool.

The new bull ruling the harem of the Golden Seal watches impassively from a distance. He has seen these kills a hundred times before. The sharp smell of blood and sweat and cigarettes, and the shouts of men, are faintly disturbing but not real cause for alarm. Nothing in his past has taught him to beware. (Somehow, he avoided his own moment of truth when he was a bachelor of killable size. Perhaps he hauled out each summer at the south end of

Tolstoi, under the cliffs where the sealers never go.) He throws his nose aloft and bends his head backward to rest it on the cushion of fat surrounding his neck. He is an aristocrat, aloof, disdaining all common events.

Now he smells the fumes of the diesel trucks as they move to the killing field for the mopping up. Workmen pitch the skins into one truck and the carcasses into another. The skins rumble away to the village, while native boys ride and bounce in delight on their rubbery mass. In the village, the carcasses are chopped by a monster machine into "sealburger" for later use in animal feed. The ululations of the chopper are the only obsequies for the dead.

✦✦✦

"IT affords to the world the finest example of the rational exploitation of any wild stock of animals," said the English zoologist Colin Bertram in admiration of the sealing business. He had come for a visit to the Pribilof Islands from Antarctica, where he had overwintered in the bleak haunts of the Weddell and crabeater seals. On the Pribilofs he talked long hours with the biologists about seal research and management.

It is rational indeed, the exploitation of the Pribilof seals, but the biologists think now of Bertram's words in a milieu where human values are changing more rapidly than ever before in history. What *is* the highest use of the seal herd? Should it be held, as it has for two centuries, as a brood stock for the production of a luxury good? Or should the seals and the beautiful islands where they live be conserved for education? for natural-history research? for tourist recreation? Though the seals are in fact contributing to all of these human needs, the question of a proper balance, or priority of use, is unresolved.

At the moment, the biologists do not question the rightness or wrongness of killing seals, as against letting nature do it alone. They do not seek an engagement of moral opinion on a matter which must, in the long run, be settled by private conscience. The man who says, while he knifes into a rare steak at dinner, that the killing of animals is "dehumanizing," has a right to his opinion.

Moreover, the value of the Pribilof seals is not a purely national concern, for Canada, Japan, and the Soviet Union are partners with the United States in a grand conservation scheme that has endured since 1911 (with some interruptions for business of war). The United States, as chief steward of the Pribilof herd, cannot, and should not, make unilateral decisions on the uses to which the seals shall be put.

+++

FAR out in Bering Sea on the third of August the Golden Seal has come to the end of her third fishing trip.

Now she is setting a turnabout course for St. Paul Island, which lies roughly east-northeast and 200 miles away. A week ago she left her pup on land and headed west toward Siberia, swimming for an hour, then riding with the current, then drifting in and out of sleep. She was impelled by an instinct common to all animals from the jelly-speck amoeba to the whale—the urge to explore without anticipation of reward. So now she tests the current with her nose and ears and picks up an odd fish now and then. She moves along, and down to the sea floor 300 feet below, and up to the surface, until she finds an attractive school of fish or squid, where she stays. She is not alone in her hunting; thousands like her are searching the waters around the Pribilofs, fishing to provide for their young.

Within the Golden Seal two conflicting urges come and go. One is the desire to remain in the feeding grounds through which she passed in other summers of her life. The other is the need to feed a hungry pup on a dark land below the horizon. How does she choose between these urges? When does she decide to turn about for land? Perhaps, when her breasts are full after a week of feeding at sea, she feels the tension and heads for home and relief through her suckling pup.

Her milk organ, or mammary gland, is most peculiar. It drapes like a thick, continuous apron beneath the skin from her heels to her armpits and part-way up the sides of her body. It holds a half-gallon of milk and yet does not distort the sleek, streamlined contour of the body, a shape essential for a swimming animal.

Thus far, the Golden Seal has enjoyed good weather. Oh, there were days when the whitecaps raced across the gray sea plain, but eastern Bering Sea is shallow, and summer winds die away as quickly as they come. In the North Pacific, though, 250 miles south of the Pribilofs, where a few of her older sisters have ventured to feed, great seas wash the wildest coasts in the world. During storms, when mountains of green water rise high and slam against the cliffs of the Aleutian Islands, the seals—and the whales and porpoises too—stay well out to sea, away from land.

The Golden Seal stretches her head and shoulders lazily above the water and treads with broad, oarlike arms as she turns her snout to the north and east. In one shooting motion she grows inches in length as the deep muscles of her neck straighten the sinuous bony column within it. The outer fur of the neck breaks open, dripping in a pattern of silver-and-black arrows like the down-pointed plumes in a waterfall. Each ear is a fur-covered tube 1½ inches long, pencil-thin, pointing stiffly backward, resembling the ear of no other animal on earth. She breathes deeply, and her round, dark, luminous eyes stare toward the skyline with each slow lift of the heaving sea. After a minute she is satisfied with the faint message brought to her nostrils, a whiff of the rank perfume compounded on the seal and seabird rookeries of her native land. Simultaneously, her brain is computing, storing away, and feeding back bits of information on water temperature, direction of the prevailing wind, position of the sun in the sky, depth of the water, and odor of the water.

Yes, *odor,* for the currents of the Arctic Ocean, the Chukchi Sea, the Sea of Okhotsk, the Sea of Japan, Bristol Bay, and the North Pacific Ocean all mingle here at one time or another. They swirl and push against each other, and the fresher ones override the saltier, unless the saltier ones are warmer, when the action is reversed. Each current carries its own peculiar burden of microscopic life— the plankton—a burden that varies in kind and quantity with the season and with a million other factors in the history of the stream.

The odors and tastes of the ocean currents are seldom identified by man. His nerve-endings in tongue and nose are grossly crude as compared with those of the seal, a beast with at least 30 million years of seafaring ancestry. Only rarely does an organism—usually a one-celled plant-animal—bloom in such uncountable numbers that man is able to smell the faintly oily, or grassy, or acrid odors given off, a few molecules at a puff, from each speck of life.

At nine in the morning the Golden Seal plunges forward and starts to swim. Her breasts are nearly full, and her stomach, for the moment, is entirely full. Four days from now she will glide into English Bay under the shadow of Tolstoi. She will swim at an average rate of 2 miles an hour, which is not to say that she will travel steadily, for she will often rest for an hour in the morning. At night, she will feed, pursuing schools of fish in bursts of speed to 15 miles an hour. Her track will be crooked, since she is not a reasoning animal and her sense of navigation, though far superior to that of a man swimming in the open sea, is incomplete.

On St. Paul Island the summer harvest is over. Fifty thousand salted skins are tucked away neatly in new wooden barrels that lie, row on row, on a pumice field near the St. Paul shipping dock. Freshly printed on the head of each barrel are the letters USA, or CANADA, or JAPAN. Fifteen out of a hundred barrels now belong to the governments of Canada and Japan, while seventy remain in ownership of the United States. This country shares the harvest with those North Pacific nations that have no rookeries, and in return those governments forbid their nationals to kill seals on the open sea.

As the harvest was drawing to a close last week on St. Paul Island, the workmen were daily more annoyed by mother seals and bulls and two-year males that swarmed among the bachelors in the roundups. The two-year-olds were the latest arrivals on the scene, fresh from the ocean, since seals habitually return to land in the order of their age, the youngest last. The old males and females among the driven animals were seals that had wandered from the rookeries after the break-up of social life in late July.

On Tolstoi, the changed pattern of life is clearly evident. Though a few harem bulls are still on station, each wearily beating a circular path around a cluster of cows, most of them have given up the struggle and are sleeping on sands at the edge of the sea a half-mile beyond the rookery. Their bodies are gaunt, their skin is wrinkled. Their places in breeding duty now are taken by younger males, some of them only six years old, who have been fretting and fuming in the background; they constitute a social caste known to the natives as the "idle bulls."

As though the rookery had been squeezed by a giant hand, through the fingers of which the pups could escape, these little fellows are now clustered in groups of their own kind. In trying to avoid the lumbering bodies of the adults they have finally found relief in association with their fellows. Here in black "pup pods" the mothers seek them out to nurse them.

When a pup's mother has been long at sea and the pup is very hungry, it may seek a pacifier—another pup in the same stage of distress—and the two will then engage in a mutual sucking bout. Curled like Yin and Yang, each will suck the dry fur of the side, or armpit, of the other.

✦✦✦

AT the edge of Tolstoi there is a clearing known as Station Thirteen. Here, on a rock the size of a piano, the number "13" was painted long ago by surveyors who mapped the outlines of all the Pribilof rookeries. The white-painted number has often been renewed, for it serves to identify a sampling place, or study plot, where the biologists return periodically to count certain classes of seals, to mark them for future study, and to photograph.

At first glance, the scene is a football field without the cheering crowd. Three biologists are grouped in the center of the field, while four black-haired natives, dripping with exertion, are driving a pod of pups. The day is bright hazy; the air is still; the Bering Sea whispers on the beach. Yellow raincoats brighten the scene with color where the men have shed them in the unaccustomed heat, now nearing 60 degrees. The pups tumble along like dark little maggots, bleating and floundering. One that has overfed relieves itself in the manner of a human baby, in a fountain of white. A biologist holding sheep shears struggles to remove a patch of fur from the top of the head of another. Though the operation is painless, the pup gives a sharp, huffy bark of indignation and dashes away, only to find itself back in the seething pool of black bodies.

Today on Tolstoi the men will shear two thousand pups. During the next fortnight, the shorn pups will mingle freely with the unshorn. Then the biologists will return to count the shorn and the unshorn together and estimate, from the ratio between the two, the number of pups that must have been present at the start of the shearing.

By noon the shearing is done. It has gone quickly in the hands of the natives: the short, cheerful men who live here from the day they are born to the day they are carried to the Russian Orthodox cemetery with its white crosses facing the seal rookeries of the Reef.

After lunch, the men take up another marking job. A truck from the village brings a carton of dry ice, or solid carbon dioxide. The men round up a hundred pups; a biologist dips a copper branding-iron in a pot of alcohol embedded in the ice and holds it for a few seconds against the rump of a pup. The subzero chill penetrates the roots of the hair and kills the cells that manufacture their black pigment. When the pup sheds its birthcoat in October and grows a handsome new gray one, it will carry for life a hieroglyphic in the shape of the brand.

The old biologist recalls a dirty week on St. Paul Island when he had to supervise the fire-branding of five thousand pups. He would never do it again. The federal Fish and Wildlife Service had been created on the last day of June that year, and in September the biologist was asked to carry out the branding as the start of a long-term program designed to reveal the vital statistics of the herd.

The St. Paul village blacksmith hammered out a set of branding irons and rigged up a portable forge. The work-men started operations on the Reef under a canvas shelter that whipped them savagely in the cold. They held rain-soaked pups against the table, one man pressing down the rump and another fighting to control the tooth-bearing end of the beast. When a third man pressed a dull-red iron against the fur, a choking cloud of steam, mingled with the smell of burnt hair and rookery filth, would rise into

42

their faces. It was all very nasty and cruel. To be sure, the biologist did see marked seals for twenty years afterward, but he had a strong suspicion that branding slowed the normal growth of the animals—a result that defeated certain purposes of the experiment.

Next year, the biologists fastened metal tags to the flippers of ten thousand seals. The tags had originally been designed for use on the ears of cattle and sheep; the special seal tags were made of stainless steel to withstand the corrosion of sea water.

Similar tags are still in use today. They are better than fire brands because they carry individual numbers and enable the biologists to track a particular seal back to the place and hour when it was marked. Most metal tags are now applied to seals older than pups, for even driving the pups, let alone handling them, brings a loss in weight and shortens life expectancy.

✦✦✦

ON the seventh of August, and again on the eighteenth, the Golden Seal returned to Tolstoi to lie beside her pup. Now she appears again in English Bay at the end of the month and the end of her fifth fishing trip. It is raining heavily. The bay is black with seals. The hauling ground is nearly deserted, for the bachelors are not dependent upon the land, and they will leave it readily when the weather turns warm or wet or when a stiff wind blows sand into their faces. Tolstoi rookery is a frightful mess. The hair of the pups is wetly parted by a white line that runs from crown to tail. The little fellows slog along, blinking to free their eyes of mud and sand and loose hairs. They crawl slowly, examining each rock as though it were new.

The Golden Seal is in no hurry to leave the bay to nurse her pup. She floats on the rolling sea until noon, by which time her last meal is digested and her stomach is clean. She rides on a slow wave to the beach and walks up the slope between the loosely spaced harems. Soon she begins to call "Baarh!" for her pup; she tests the air and turns her head back and forth. But she gets no answer.

Is her baby one of those dark, putrid things with sloughing patches of white, like the thing over there being used for a pillow by a mother seal? She snaps at a hungry pup that tries to nuzzle as she climbs the hill. She searches for an hour near a rock where the faint, familiar scent of her own baby clings, then falls asleep.

Meanwhile, her pup is trying to work his way up from the water's edge to the resting place. He is fresh and alert, and keenly hungry. He has taught himself to swim! Three weeks ago, while his mother was away, he followed an older half-brother to a quiet cove where the red and brown seaweeds of the beach and those of the sea are often intertwined. The older animal plunged in boldly and began to play with a bit of weed, tearing and tossing it with his teeth as though he were catching a fish. The pup hesitated until a wave rolled him gently into the slimy bed. He sneezed, fought wildly, and scrambled to the safety of the upper beach. Here he stayed for long minutes, watching the older pups twisting in the shallows and playing King of the Castle. On the smooth dome of a boulder rising above the water a pup would crouch until another attacked him from the rear, sending him down with a great splash.

The Golden Seal's pup at last took heart and began to paddle in the water. Exhilaration and a sense of fulfillment must have flooded his being. Here at the water's edge he stayed until the tide turned, and here he came again and again for three weeks to sport with the damp brotherhood.

So today at the end of August the pup is hungry and is striving to reach the nursery. He circles the edge of Tolstoi and is attacked by a "salacious bachelor." He squirms away in the mud and runs uphill on a long slant to the place where he last saw his mother. Here she is sleeping. She wakens with a snarl when he butts her in the belly, then the pair curl together warmly while the rain drums on the rocks and the sky darkens imperceptibly into the summer night.

✦✦✦

SOMETIMES a popular magazine will contain an article stating that the mother seal "teaches" her young one to swim. Now, a pup may try frantically to climb on the back of an older seal. One could easily say, "It's his mother, and she's forcing him to learn," but it would not be true.

When the old biologist first went to the islands he was told the fable of the swimming lesson, so he went to Tolstoi, found a newborn female pup with a fresh umbilical cord, and dropped her into one of the deep, saltwater tanks used for washing skins. She swam furiously for twenty minutes, with head high and body trailing deep. She was not fat enough to be buoyant, but she did know how to swim. He took compassion, and returned her to her mother. When he passed by an hour later he picked her up in his arms for a moment and set her down. She was fast asleep and did not waken.

SEPTEMBER

The Golden Seal and her pup have wandered away from the rookery and are resting on a fragrant bed of white-and-green chickweed. The pup lies limply on his side, with his hind flippers pointing forward and his front ones draped over them. His belly again bulges with milk; he is a neat, round package of content. In the first two months of life he has grown from his newborn weight of 10 pounds to 22. Washes of silvery color on the sides of his face and along his belly tell that his black birthcoat is molting fast. If he were not so sleepy, he would scratch. Other pups are strewn about like driftwood. Some lie on their backs on the sand; some hang over rocks in awkward angles as though they had chosen their beds in the dark. Many are scratching at lice fastened to their ears or clustered around their body openings. A gaunt orphan with crusted tears rimming its eyes, and with ribs showing, moves to the Golden Seal and nurses hungrily for a minute at her nipples. She rouses, turns, and gives him a savage bite that throws him off. Two pups are playing tug-of-war. They pull ferociously on a rope of dried seaweed, in the fibers of which one of them leaves embedded the last of his baby teeth.

Above a corner of the rookery known to the natives as "The Death Trap," a faint, sickly odor hangs in the late summer day. Here, long ago, giant boulders came to rest in a pattern of dark crevasses, and here a pup sometimes falls to his death. His voice will be heard for a week; his mother will peer anxiously into the gloom and finally will wander away.

The Golden Seal yawns, sniffs the wind, and drags her brown body down the slope. She pauses beside another female in her path, a cow in labor, about to give birth to a large, late-season pup. This one has picked a poor couch in a jumble of rocks. She makes no sound, though she seems to be in pain. She lies down, rises, then nuzzles her tail and makes a full circle. When she has made three circles, a copious discharge of fluid stains the sand, and the black tail of a pup appears at her opening. She sways her hindquarters back and forth—back and forth. Six minutes later the pup is free. She gives a shrill, trumpeting bawl, not a call of triumph but the release of an inborn urge to start communication with this new life come suddenly from hiding. The pup is quiet; it stares unblinkingly. Its body lies like a wet rag on the ground; its fore flippers lie outward passively like the wings of an airplane. The mother seizes it roughly with her teeth and shakes it. She is a big, strong cow, over 100 pounds in weight. The pup rises to its feet and begins to stagger on the sand, coughing and bleating feebly.

The Golden Seal moves on but is again interrupted. Where the slope of Tolstoi levels off she is startled by two men in brown who materialize from the brown rocks. They rush toward her and one of them deftly drops a coil of rope over her head—a rope fastened to a wooden pole.

He twists the pole in his hands and the noose chokes her. The second one starts to shove her rump into a burlap bag, when he pauses and points. "Nipples—she's nursing. Let her go." He backs away, and the man with the pole turns his head to look around for an escape route, then releases the Golden Seal. She strikes quickly, leaving a crimson gash on his thumb, then lunges toward the sea in frantic leaps.

The men are natives of St. Paul out to capture three small seals for California Institute. Each summer they are called upon to furnish live seals for zoos, aquariums, and research institutions. Later this morning they have no trouble in filling their quota. Then they put the seals into aluminum crates and truck them to the village. With pans of fresh water, but no food, the captives leave the island by air at one o'clock. On the following noon, they will smell the soft odors of eucalyptus in San Francisco Bay.

A week after the capture of the seals, the native who was bitten is painfully reminded of the accident. His thumb swells and stiffens and turns dark purplish red. He visits the infirmary, where the doctor gives him a shot and says, "You've got fat-finger." The man has never suffered this ailment before. The doctor says that it's a kind of blood poisoning, an occupational disease that affects the sealers of Scandinavia but is rare in America. The pain disappears after a month, though the joint of the thumb will never again be as flexible as it was.

+ + +

AT California Institute, the three captured seals are dumped on a concrete ramp at the edge of a circular pool. A trainer watches in satisfaction as they plunge into the pool and circle for minutes before they rise, bubbling. They give no sign of distress at finding themselves in a saltless sea. They do give signs of interest in animals beyond the fence, for here, in a large enclosure, are elephant seals, California sea lions, Steller sea lions, and harbor seals, all together in a peaceable kingdom. A monotone rises from a bull sea lion who must forever assert his dominance by honking "Ount! ount! ount! ount!" Some of the seals are stretched prone on the concrete, baking their brains in the sun, while others are playing in a green pool. Under a shady tree, a girl in coveralls is feeding a seal pup through a stomach tube— a pretty girl in spite of her red, sweaty face all splattered with milk.

At California Institute, or rather, at this small unit called the Seal Facility, special studies of the physiology and behavior of pinnipeds are carried on throughout the year. The staff members have adopted a thoughtful approach to the handling of experimental animals; they tame each one before they test it. A tame seal, they reason, will perform on command a task that would leave a wild one in a lather of exhaustion. Moreover, the wild seal, frightened and tense, would deliver an abnormal performance.

In an "anechoic chamber"—a pool with muted walls in a pitch-dark room—a specialist is timing Freddy, a young fur seal, at the task of capturing fish thrown into the pool. Some are live mudsuckers and others are dead herring; all were counted before they were offered to him. Those remaining uneaten will be counted when the lights are again turned on. Freddy is an orphan yearling raised at the Facility in isolation from other seals. He proves to be surprisingly adept at finding the fish in total darkness in an average time of seven seconds per fish, or just as quickly as when the pool was brightly lit. What is his secret? An ultrasound recorder suspended in the water of the pool gives evidence of a steady barrage of inaudible "clicks" produced by the motion of his body. Though he glides like silk in utter silence, millions of tiny bubbles no larger than a pinhead are forming and collapsing in the faint turbulence at the interface of his body and the water. Their collapse is a sound more familiar than rain to Freddy's hypersensitive ears. Using his innate ability to echo-locate—there were no older seals to teach him—he senses the direction, the distance, the size, and the texture of the fish upon which he preys.

In another pool a psychologist is giving a similar test, though here to a sea lion working in full daylight, speeding on command toward a pair of visual, rather than acoustic, targets. The patient experimenter, wearing a green eyeshade, sits on a high stool at the end of the pool. He challenges the animal by replacing the targets with other pairs that look increasingly alike. Finally, when the targets differ by only 6 percent in area, and the animal can make no better choice than 50-50, he calls a halt and gives it a performance rating.

The veterinarians (the medical staff) of the Facility are forever trying to find better ways to keep seals healthy. Though the laboratory care of common animals —dogs, cats, chickens, white rats—is well understood, the care of seals is chancy. A simple question like "How do you feed an orphan pup?" would seem to have a ready answer: "Why, you give it canned milk and fish oil." But the veterinarians know that this is not the right answer. Natural seal milk contains almost no sugar, and to feed an orphan seal on cow's milk, which contains 5 percent, may kill it with kindness.

The men of the Facility are seldom free from the vexing problems of *apparatus*—of instruments to be invented or modified for use on slippery, agile, amphibious beasts. (An elephant seal can touch its rump with the back of its head!) How does one attach a radio transmitter to a seal to follow its movements? They have tried, with poor-to-fair success, metal clips, buttons, sutures through the skin, collars, and girdles. They have concealed a miniature transmitter in a herring and fed the herring to a seal, but the transmitter functioned for only a few hours. One of the men is now experimenting with an intrauterine coil, similar to a contraceptive loop, which he is implanting in a sea lion. Attached to the coil is a small transmitter that steadily announces the cardiac potential of the host.

In a tree-shaded pen at the Facility, a harbor seal known as Tuffy is revealing the velocity of his blood, though all he knows of the matter is that he woke this morning from a very deep sleep to find a harness round his neck. Within his body, planted aseptically while he lay unconscious, there is now a plastic tube with a device that sends out ultrasound from one wall of an artery to another. With each pulse of the heart, the sound rises and falls and the message is translated by a tiny radio in the harness and picked up 20 feet away by an FM receiver. "Lub-dup ... lub-dup ... lub-dup ..." says the heart as the electronic waves ebb and flow and a new page is written in the story of man's effort to understand the dynamics of life, to measure the vast difference between a dead seal and a live one.

At Tolstoi on the tenth of September the black trucks of the biology crew again wind their way through the sand dunes and come to a halt within walking distance of the rookery. The biologists are pleased to find that the day is cool and dry, for this is the day when they will weigh the pups. The leader climbs to the crest of a dune and scans the tundra to see where the animals are resting. Satisfied, he beckons to the gang and they move off through tall grass that ripples to their knees. They aim for an isolated group of five hundred pups and a hundred nursing mothers. Crouching as they walk, they close the distance, then rise and run at full speed to surround the animals. The mothers stream toward the beach, while the pups mill in confusion, trying to climb upon one another or to bury their noses in a pile. A warm vapor rises from their bodies. As the first panic ebbs, they quiet down in sound and motion. Within ten minutes, the biologists are able to seize one pup at a time by its hind flippers and drag it, snarling, over the grass to a man who stands on a platform scale. Man and seal are weighed as one; the man's weight will be subtracted later.

Today's performance is an effort to get evidence on "body condition." The average weight of a seal varies slightly from year to year for reasons yet unknown. Presumably the pup is fatter when the weather has been milder, and when the nursing mothers have been able to find food closer to the rookeries. In any case, the biologists hope some day to use the fatness factor to predict the survival of a year-class. The first winter at sea is a cruel one; more than half of the pups die and the survivors barely hold their own. At the age of sixteen months they weigh little more than they did at four months, when they left the land.

Today at Tolstoi, four hundred pups are weighed in three hours. This being the quota for the rookery, the men rest on the grass and watch the swirling white clouds, and argue. The issue of the moment is whether the Alaska seal was or was not a larger animal in the old days of pelagic sealing when the herd was uncrowded—when it was only one-eighth its present size. The record shows that the bachelors, at least, are smaller than they used to be, though one of the men claims that the record is not to be trusted. "You've pushed the argument far beyond the available evidence," he insists.

Another discussion turns on the question: Why did the herd stop growing in the early 1940s? The men agree that rookery space could hardly have been a limiting factor, for the Pribilof Islands have many vacant beaches. The food supply of the mothers is a probability. That is to say, as the herd increased, the competition for food among the hundreds of thousands of nursing mothers grew keener; the average mother had to swim farther from the islands to find fish and squid; she returned less frequently to feed her baby; the pup put on less weight; more pups died in their first year; and the herd decreased. Such may have been the circular chain of cause and effect that governed the rise and fall of the seal population.

Quite surely, though, the biological lines of force that pull and haul at the seals in their every living moment are a web of such complexity that no model contrived by the mind of man can explain the slow, drifting changes in the size of the multitude. First-year mortality at sea is perhaps not the most important effect of undernourishment during the suckling period. The stunted pup may in fact live through this critical year but never catch up with its normal class mates. If it is a female, its attainment of puberty will be delayed, it will have a shorter reproductive life, and its own pups will tend to be smaller, or more often aborted, than the pups dropped by normal mothers.

THE cool wind dies and a hush settles over Tolstoi. The Golden Seal is suddenly warm. She waves her hind flippers in the air and pants with mouth open, and sheds tears that spill down her cheeks, since seals have no duct from eye to nose. Her sleek jacket folds in accordion pleats as she bites in irritation at an itch on her rump. A short distance away, a late-born pup with umbilical cord attached to its belly pulls feebly to free itself from a trap: a bull is standing on the cord and placenta and is paying no attention to the struggle. A mother fans herself with a flipper and rhythmically slaps her baby in the face; he does not have sense enough to move out of range.

The pup of the Golden Seal scratches constantly. He moves to mother for comfort. He lifts his head and slides his chin along her throat, trying to reach her nose. As she bends in a gentle motion, the white profile of her fur, transilluminated from nose to back, defines a perfect arc.

The storm strikes from the north. Long before the usual hour of twilight the icy darkness presses down. At some time during the night the wind shifts to the east, and before it has spent its fury on the evening of the second day it turns to the southeast and lashes the face of the village. At Marunich, on the north shore, the seas build to a force that can only be learned later by the evidence of drift logs high on the tundra. At Northeast Point, a wooden hut used by fox trappers is carried away and never seen again. In the tower of the church the bells ring through the night, while sand flows under the village doors and through the keyholes and into the eyes of the night-watchman bending into the gale.

The foxes stay curled in their underground dens; the gulls huddle on the mudflats in the lee of shoreline tussocks, with their yellow bills pointing in one direction. The reindeer, too, face the wind, as is their custom, until it reaches a screaming force that makes them leave the plain and climb a well-worn trail to the shelter of the old volcanic crater on Lake Hill.

But the seal pups have few places to hide. Some of them poke their noses among the rocks; a few find volcanic caves where they lie with big eyes mirroring the pale light. Some of the June pups are strong enough to swim from point to point, where they find uneasy rest in the churning kelp. Many pups are caught by the breakers and drowned. The pup of the Golden Seal weathers the storm on an open field of beaten grass. When daylight comes he is a seedy creature indeed, his fur ruffled and patched with white shell-sand and bits of vegetation.

✦✦✦
✦✦✦

ON the Sunday after the storm, the natives go beach-combing. They pass by the carcasses of the pups, the poor familiar things half buried or washed in rows along the drift. The gulls have taken their eyes, the living seals have trod upon them, and the foxes have pulled their entrails into long pink ribbons that lead to nowhere. Here and there, windrows of torn seaweed are knee-deep on the strand—redolent, squishy, filled with small invertebrate life. Lengths of fish-netting from the Japanese and Soviet fleets of the Bering Sea are strewn about. They are hazardous to seals, for their nylon webbing may trap the neck of a swimming animal, choking him or eventually starving him. The natives see in great variety the glass balls that float the nets. Some are larger than a basketball and would bring twenty dollars in a curio shop in Seattle.

Here the storm has undercut a sandy cliff along the shore and has laid bare the bones of a walrus, complete with so-called fossil ivory, which is only the tusk material stained in rich colors of coffee and cream.

A native recalls that once, when he walked the beach, he stooped and picked up a tooth of a hairy mammoth, a corrugated tooth the size of a grapefruit. It may have fallen from the mucky bank of some mainland stream to an ice floe which rafted it later to the Pribilofs.

Or the ancient elephant may have walked in life to what is now the Pribilofs during a glacial stage when the world sea level was lower than it is now and the islands were part of the land bridge between Asia and America.

Though the biologists estimate the loss of Tolstoi pups in the storm at 3,000, they presume that some were weak or sickly at the start. Wind and sea brought them to a merciful end. This is not to say that all storms are a blessing, for cold wet winds that strike in July take the strong as well as the weak. The forces of nature wax and wane in their impact. One summer on the Pribilofs the biologists counted 120,000 pups dying from all causes; another summer, only 17,000.

In the bright autumn days that follow the storm the biologists and the natives are busy at many tasks. Deployed in a skirmish line, they walk the length of sampling grounds where they count the dead pups each summer. As each man finds a carcass, he marks it with a pinch of white powder so that he won't count it twice.

Rarely, he finds the body of a pup prematurely born, a naked pink little thing that was dropped, for one reason or other, at the wrong time of year. One man contends that a "preemie" seal is the runt of a pair of twins. Another holds that something went wrong with the mother's physiology, causing her body to suppress the development of the fetus until late winter, by which time it could not catch up with its classmates.

As the biologists count the casualties of the summer

they also stop to examine the bodies of older seals found dead. This is a nasty job, for some have been dead for several months. From the skull of each they cut a tooth for later study in the lab, when they will count the growth rings and estimate the age. The main point of the study of older seals is to get evidence on the "rate of replacement," or turnover, among breeding bulls and also to estimate the annual mortality. With a knowledge of mortality rates by age and sex, they can draw up a kind of life-insurance table which will lead to an understanding of herd size and composition.

Today, the men find that most of the bull carcasses are those of animals nine to eleven years old, and that most of them died from wounds caused by fighting. Throughout the whole range of ages, or seven to seventeen years, the yearly death rate is 40 percent, a rate which is very high, as compared with the rate among human males of breeding age.

On the rookery called Kitovi, within sight of Tolstoi, two of the biologists are setting free a bachelor seal on whose body a nylon harness now carries a radio transmitter. Seven other seals burdened in like fashion are roaming the island, but four of them have ceased reporting in —their radios have developed leaks in the wet climate. The purpose of the telemetering study is to trace the movements of the seals. The men are asking, for example, "When a bachelor is driven to a killing field and is then allowed to go free, does he leave the island in fright or does he forget his rude experience and return to the hauling ground?" In late September, some of the older pups swim from one rookery to another. How, then, does the mother find her pup to nurse it? Does the pup come home for dinner? Is a nomad pup one that has lost its mother? Why does the male seal come to the island anyway during the summers long before he is able to breed?

On their way to the village, the biologists stop to watch a flock of gulls dipping and rising in excitement a quarter-mile off the Reef. Through glasses, they see the black triangular fins of killer whales—at least four and maybe more—moving in steady file toward the west. The gulls are feeding on scraps of food torn and left by the whales, but the nature of the food cannot be distinguished at a distance.

"I have never understood," says one of the men, "why we don't see more killers here in summer. With several hundred thousand pups learning to swim, you would think they would be easy prey. As I recall, old Captain Bryant found eighteen pups in the stomach of one killer, and twenty-four in another."

"Boloney," is the answer. "I've traced that story to a sailor's yarn from Newfoundland. I think a seal can turn and twist and dive so much quicker than a whale that the whale finally gets discouraged—like a coyote after a rabbit in the sagebrush."

One biologist mentions that a native reported seeing big chunks of seal meat, and dying seals, on a beach where killers had just gone by offshore. The others agree that killers do indeed capture and eat seals of many species, but why they do not exploit the waters of the Pribilofs in summer must remain for the time a mystery.

✦ˆ✦ˆ✦

ON the last day of September the Golden Seal is 300 miles north of the Islands of Four Mountains and two days from Tolstoi, homeward bound near the end of her eighth fishing trip. Silently the gray sea rises and falls. The long swells roll away toward the east where they disappear in a pale shimmering promise of dawn. Around seven o'clock the sun dimly shows its place in the sky, then for the rest of the day hides in a blanket above the lead-gray sea. The peeping of sandpipers and their summer chicks is the only sound in the air. The little brown-and-gray birds are forever picking at invisible points on the water.

A sudden *p-aahf* breaks the silence as the Golden Seal rises dripping with a mouthful of small fish, their tails hanging from her lips. She blows her nose and shakes her head in a froth of motion, then tosses the broken fish into the air and catches them in her open mouth as they fall. Her white teeth flash, and the fish are down. The sandpipers break in alarm but soon return to their busywork of doing nothing at all. A shearwater glides in stiffly from somewhere in the gray mist and settles to the surface near the seal, hoping to steal a scrap of food, but nothing remains but a rain of silver scales descending.

A cold meal out of a cold sea at 48 degrees, with the prospect of a nap soon in a cold wet bed—what a life the Golden Seal must lead! But in fact she is warm and content. Her jacket of fur is woven of fibers so fine that 300,-000 are packed in a square inch and, moreover, they are curly and waterproof. In effect, her body warmth is contained by an insulating blanket of billions of air spaces. The surface of her skin is always dry.

As she penetrates one salty ocean stream after another she feels the temperatures that identify the water masses from various sources in the northern hemisphere. She is in Bering Sea. When later she will cut across the great bend of the North Pacific on migration, she will travel for hours in deep waters that are uniformly cool. They are cool, at least, down to the limit of her diving range.

She has been fishing leisurely since midnight for a food with a strange history. It is a kind of deep-sea smelt. It was first known in the 1890s from bones found in fur-seal stomachs and was given the name "seal fish." It was not seen again for seventy years, and then biologists collecting in Bering Sea were surprised to find its remains in the stomachs of many seals. A few intact fish—gulped only minutes before the seal met its fate—enabled the men to identify it as a deep-sea smelt which, though never seen alive, had been known to science for a long time.

On this fishing trip, as on most of her trips, the Golden Seal is alone, though she is often aware of companions feeding nearby. She hears their underwater murmur. On quiet days she may loaf at the surface in a group of three or four, and sometimes she finds herself among a dozen, all pursuing the same school of fish. The true social life of the seals is lived on land. Neither in feeding nor in defense against a common enemy, such as a shark, do they ever find advantage in joining forces at sea.

The Golden Seal becomes aware, even in the morning darkness, of something noisy and smelly hovering at the northern edge of her feeding ground. Daylight shows a fishing vessel drifting on the swell: an eighty-foot gillnetter, battered and grimy from weeks at sea. After breakfast her crew will haul the net that hangs unseen, like a curtain a quarter-mile long, from floats on the surface.

The Golden Seal is wary but not alarmed, for she has often seen and smelled the machines of men. She swims idly toward the vessel, keeping her body below the surface and stroking evenly with her long black flippers. She rises at intervals of a minute or two to breathe. Within a hundred yards of the vessel she sees a splendid king salmon twisting in what seems to be a tangle of seaweed. (It is in fact the webbing of the great net.) She darts toward the fish, turns on her side, tears a mouthful of red meat from its belly, and wheels in a circle. Back again, she grabs the tail and pulls the mutilated body from the net.

The net itself she dodges by luck rather than skill. Though she has seen the drowned bodies of other seals hanging from nets, she learned no lesson from the sight.

Rising to the surface, the Golden Seal plays with the fish, splashing mightily, tearing bits and letting them fly. She lets the carcass sink, then strikes it from beneath with such force that she clears the surface in a flashing arc, in a fountain of black and white.

Thud! A heavy impact strikes the water from all directions. It is followed in a split second by the boom of a heavy rifle. In a frantic lunge of power the Golden Seal puts all swimming organs into play—her flippers fore and aft, and her muscular body. Down she goes in a boil of green, and away toward the whispering sands of Tolstoi.

OCTOBER

At the upper edge of Tolstoi there is a cavern where, long ago, the surface of a lava stream congealed at the instant when the mother lode of molten rock drained off through another channel. Now the cavern is a fairy place of mysterious shapes and dark crannies, silent and solitary, a nesting place for snowbirds and a shelter for fox puppies that sneak along its floor in the dim shade of grasses and sweet angelica. Rock ferns and lilies-of-the-valley, protected from the wind, grow deeper and deeper into the musty gloom until they fade into tender-leaf green and finally disappear.

Early in October the Golden Seal is searching for her pup, and he too is searching for her. They meet at last at the entrance to this cavern. She knows him by voice and odor, but not at first by sight. In her absence he has been transformed; the black pup is now silver. During the first thirteen weeks of life (and even earlier, in the womb) his coat was changing from the simple pattern of fibers that form the coat of a dog or a cat to a complicated structure unique to fur seals. It now contains bundles of fur fibers, twenty or more in a bundle, each bundle protected by a stiff guard hair. The guard-hair layer, not the fur beneath it, gives the seal his outward look.

Never will the pup be more handsome than now, as he stands erect by the cavern in his shining coat. Along his back from snout to rump he is lustrous gray; his chest and belly are nearly white. Two light cheeks, with dark-rimmed eyes and black mustaches, are a domino mask. A pale streak on each hip marks him as a youngster; these will disappear in adolescence three or four years from now. His pelage is new and alive; the tips of the hairs are sharp and clean, unworn, unsoiled.

In another way he shows that he has come of age: all his wisdom teeth have erupted through the gums. In a human child, the appearance of wisdom teeth at thirteen weeks would suggest sorcery. But the young seal must telescope its growth during the four months allotted to its nursing, so that it can survive the crashing break in November from the comfort of the nursery to the awful, empty wildness of the North Pacific Ocean.

Below the Golden Seal and her pup, among the boulders, and on the sand, and on the tundra, and on driftwood and fermenting piles of kelp, and on redolent mats of sageweed, ten thousand fat pups are sleeping or playing. Five thousand more are swimming in the surf, or are paddling between the water and the beach. Where the long green swells rise majestically to breaking white, the pups hang for an instant, framed in translucent walls.

Off to the northwest, at the base of a rough hill called Kaminista—the Rocky Place—thousands of birds are gorging on a special food of the late summer season. They have dropped down to St. Paul on their southward journey after nesting above the Arctic Circle. The older birds remember the Pribilofs and the special food they find here. They always stop in the fall; their offspring learn the habit, as will their offspring in turn.

So down through all the years since the coming of man and the killing of seals in summer, the birds have learned to stop for a few days to feed on the blowfly maggots that wriggle from the naked bodies of the dead seals. Most of the bodies are taken to the sealburger factory, but once in a while the kill of the day is too great to handle—4,000 or even 5,000 animals. Then the surplus carcasses are dumped from a cliff into the sea or are trucked to some tundra hollow to be scavenged by the birds, the foxes, and the lesser forms of animal life. The golden plovers and the ruddy turnstones are feeding now on the brown fields at Kaminista. A pile of carcasses, two months old, is very, very ripe.

In flocks of hundreds, the plovers pick at the tundra moss, turning out the maggots and the brown pupa cases. A fox approaches, and they fly to the hillside, protesting "Wheedle! wheedle!"

The golden plover is called an aristocrat among birds for its stately manner, its rich yellow mantle, black breast, and streamers of white from forehead to shoulders. It grows buttery fat on maggots and then moves on to Hawaii, or the South Sea islands, or even deeper into the southern hemisphere.

Mingling freely with the plovers are hosts of ruddy turnstones, beautiful shorebirds with harlequin bodies and orange legs. They rise from the ground with ruptive patterns of display and chattering voices. Like the plovers, they gorge until their bodies are bedded deep in yellow fat, then set off in small groups for lands below the skyline.

✦✦✦

ON a bright Sunday morning in mid-October the chief biologist of St. Paul Island hikes out to the Reef to photograph the seal groupings. The first freezing weather of autumn came last night and brought a quick shower of hail. The white pellets are melting in the morning sun. The Reef is a mile-long peninsula on whose beaches the fur seals breed in three extensive rookeries. The biologist walks along the central ridge, while foxes trail him at a safe distance, yapping disapproval. (The petulant voice of the blue fox is very annoying until one learns to smile at it.) He passes a sign beside a truck-trail: CAUTION—SEAL CROSSING! It is surely unique in all the world. At a place called the Tower, he sets his camera on a rock and looks down at the shifting scene before him. Black and brown and gray, the seals cover the beach and move among the slippery boulders and fade into the distance.

But those pups at the base of the Tower—why do they stagger so? He shoulders his camera and picks his way down a gully to a parade ground where hundreds of gray pups are resting. At this season, few pups should be dying, but here are dozens of dead and wounded. He wonders: Did a bull go berserk and attack them? Were they caught in a rock-slide?

With the big knife he always carries at his belt, he cuts into several bodies. Evidently the pups were healthy when they died a day or two ago. Soon he sees a common feature: all the wounds are on top of the head and all were inflicted by a heavy object. He sees small footprints in the sand. They are human footprints.

Troubled, he returns to the village. How shall he deal with the situation? He calls at the home of two native boys, brothers, who are his special friends. They often watch him at work in the laboratory, where they offer to run errands and to help him hold his instruments. "Yes," the older one says, "we know the kids who did it; we saw them out there yesterday." When the full story is revealed, nine children are implicated in the clubbing of four hundred pups. The youngest "delinquent" is only six years old. With broom handles and driftwood clubs they slipped away from the village on Saturday morning and, screened by the Tower, carried out a busy little sealing drive in imitation of their elders. In a sense, they should not be blamed, but the biologist suggests a punishment. The children and their parents go to the Reef, gather up the bodies, and carry them to a truck for disposal. The bright Sunday sun is low in the sky when they finish.

On the following day another biologist walks the beach of English Bay where scores of bulls, retired from harem duty on Tolstoi, are sleeping on the sand. Some of them have gone without food or drink for as long as eleven weeks. They sleep profoundly, snoring, with eyes closed. They shift their bodies from time to time without waking. He wonders idly why they stay here on land instead of returning to the ocean to feed. Perhaps it is because they are undergoing the annual molt, when millions of old hairs are being replaced. The change of life in the deep follicles of the skin must surely generate a vast fatigue. The biologist tiptoes to within four paces of a 300-pound bull and stands quietly beside him. The nose of the beast twitches when he catches a whiff of man scent. The thumping of his heart is plainly visible as a pulse beneath the brown skin. The man jots down a record of the pulse at fifty beats per minute, and the breathing rate at ten. The black, leathery nostrils remain shut most of the time; they open quickly to exhale and inhale in less than a second.

The respiratory pattern resembles that of a whale and is an adaptation for breathing at sea, where all marine mammals must perpetually defend themselves against the very liquid that supports their life. When a man holds his breath, he operates the muscles that lie at the back of his throat. The seal does the same, but he also pinches his outer nostrils like a valve. When a seal is found dead in captivity at the bottom of a pool, its lungs are not full of water. This is evidence of an automatic cutoff which begins to operate as the seal lapses into unconsciousness.

The skin of the bull is loose and wrinkled. He has lost 60 pounds in two months of breeding duty. How can I measure this loss, the man wonders. He knows that it has never been done. He could estimate the loss by figuring the caloric budget, knowing that the animal's food in summer is drawn from its own body fat and muscle. Or he could start in May with a bull newly arrived from the ocean, drug it from a distance with a dart-syringe, erect a tripod on the beach and suspend the immobilized animal by tackle from a weighing scale, mark its back with a splash of orange paint, and leave it to waken. By repeating this performance at ten-day intervals throughout the breeding season, he could plot the weight loss. He shudders at the thought of manhandling a bull in late June when it would be surrounded by acres of harem cows and angry bulls. Moreover, the drug would affect the bull's libido, dampen his aggressive spirit, and weaken his ability to hold status as a beachmaster. No, the only way to measure weight loss would be to kill a number of sample animals throughout the breeding season and carry them off the rookery to weigh them. A measure of the average loss would substitute for a measure of the individual loss. His conclusion is one familiar to zoologists. A physiological study in depth is seldom feasible; a study in breadth is the compromise which the researcher must usually accept.

 At lunch in the village with his colleagues he raises a question that occurred to him while he watched the beating of the bull's heart: how would one measure deep-body temperature? The group agrees finally that it could best be done by killing the subject. The consensus is followed by an uneasy silence. No better ideas are forthcoming, so two of the biologists and a native helper take a .243 rifle off the rack and set out for Lukanin, a rookery whose topography offers excellent hiding places for a sniper. The first victim is a cow sleeping in the shade of a driftwood stump. Within thirty seconds of the impact of the bullet, a man rushes to her side and places quick-acting thermometers deep within her body, one directly into the heart through a knife-puncture and others into body openings. The men repeat the operation on seals of other ages and of both sexes until they have a fair cross-section of temperature values.

In the evening, they discuss their findings in relation to human temperatures. The bulls and cows at rest that day had an average deep-body temperature of 99.9 degrees; man's daytime temperature is about 98.5. The pups were warmer than the older seals, with an average temperature of 100.8. One biologist turns to a record, taken last July during the sealing season, of seals that died in the drives from overheating and fatigue. Though the sealers are careful to drive the animals slowly, once in a while, especially when the tundra is dry, a seal will fall beside the way and will be entered in the daily log as a "roadskin." The deep temperature of a fallen animal may reach 111 degrees, though even 106 is critical. In man, the critical high is around 115.

ON the twenty-fifth of October the Golden Seal comes in from the sea toward a homeland dusted white with snow. The water currents have carried her well to the north; her first sight of land is the pale tip of Polovina reflecting level with the black sea. The landfall causes her to quicken her pace; she swims strongly toward the shore of Northeast Point; she has to skirt half the island before she can reach her goal. Her tenth fishing trip has been a long and cold one. She crosses the outer reef between the breakers, turns to the right, and finds herself once more in the misty, musty atmosphere of her native land.

Hardly has she fixed her vision on the western sky when she hears sharp gunfire coming from the beach and echoing from the bluffs of Hutchinson Hill. She has heard the sound before. She reacts in fright, increases her speed to 12 miles an hour, and continues on her course to Tolstoi.

Behind her, knee-deep in the surf, a native casts a wooden block, studded with hooks and fastened to a line. He snags the fat brown body of a floating sea lion pup and hauls it to the beach. Though the pup was born in June, it already weighs over 100 pounds and is the size of a four-year bachelor fur seal. A fine pup, thinks the native;

four nice roasts, a brisket, two meals of liver, and a tasty dish of heart, brain, and tongue. He has been shivering here all day, hoping that a sea lion of edible size would swim within range of his rifle. The biggest sea lions weigh over a ton, and their flesh is impossibly tough, dark, and doggy in flavor.

ON Kitovi rookery a weary young man is sitting in a little house only 6 feet square. It is an observation hut secured with cables to a rocky bench that overlooks the rookery. Though tiny, it has a proper door, a roof, and a view window. Here, for several hours a day, for three summers, he has watched the comings and goings of the seals, the births and deaths, the fights and courtships. He sits pensively with chin cupped in hand, for he is about to leave the Pribilofs forever. At last he gathers up his notebook and binoculars, and leaves the hut. He beats his gloved hands in the chill, turns, and waves farewell.

It seems very long ago that he stood for the first time on the cliff above Kitovi, bewildered at the sight of the swarming animals and not a little discouraged at the prospect of studying their behavior. How could he ever document the summer calendar of events, the procession of life on the rookery? How could he recognize the individual in the crowd? How could he clock its movements on land and in the sea fog into which it would disappear at intervals? He knew, then, that he would have to adopt a case-history approach, as do the sociologist and the psychologist, and would have to tag individual seals and geographic areas on the rookery.

In early spring of the next year, before the bulls arrived, he laid out a grid pattern of red-and-yellow painted rocks on several acres of rookery space. As the breeding males and females came in from the ocean, he marked selected ones by metal tags, or by a splash of paint or dye, or by a hair bleach purchased at a beauty parlor, or by a naked patch shorn with sheep shears. He had to drug the harem bulls by dart-syringe before he could handle them. Some seals with peculiar scars or color patterns did not need to be marked; they wore, in effect, natural identification tags. In one way or another, he was able at last to identify and record the movements of several hundred seals. When a certain seal hauled out from a fishing trip on a certain trip, he duly noted the fact.

He could not follow the movements of the seals at night, but he could project the daytime observations to cover the hours of darkness. On a part of the rookery that he watched for only six hours a day, or one-quarter of the twenty-four, he saw ten matings, and he counted thirty-nine pups born. If he had been on watch all twenty-four he should have seen forty matings, or virtually the same number as the pups born. This was evidence, he reasoned, that a cow copulates only once during the summer.

His observation studies were time-consuming and expensive but, once done, they were done; they yielded bench-mark data of great value. The habits of the seals are not likely to change in the near future.

Now, behind him on the airstrip of St. Paul, a team of five anthropologists is landing. They have come from eastern universities, intent on visiting corners of America where they can find fragments of old cultures, heritage remains of human ways of life that soon will be gone forever. Through study of the dead and the dying they hope to understand the ways of the living. They feel the swirl of history; they try to pin down in their own time a picture of the days when the Old Ones lived.

During the last days of October they take measurements and photographs of the Aleut-Russians of the Fur Seal Islands. They look at teeth; they record the color of skin, hair, and eyes; they test blood for special pigments and chromosomes. They tape-record a few snatches of the Aleut tongue (Pribilof variety), but only a few, because the natives are more facile in modern speech than in the language of their fathers.

"Would it be possible," a scientist finally asks, "to dig into the graves of the oldest ones to measure the changes that have taken place in the last century, to measure the accumulation of pesticides and nuclear fallout products now present in every living person?"

"We are sorry," replies the courteous president of the native council. "These are our grandfathers and great-grandfathers. The remains are those of Christians."

OCTOBER

   THE Golden Seal climbs slowly to a slanting table of
rock. She rises for a long moment on the heels of her
hands, a statue carved by a creator patient beyond infin-
ity. Her eyes are fixed on the far, empty sea; they smolder
darkly and reflect in crescents the blue curve of the sky.
She seems lost in revery. Perhaps for an instant in her
rude, reflexive life, in some small and quiet corner of her
brain, memories have collected to generate a rational
thought. Then a breeze lighter than half a feather touches
her face. The spark dies. Her whiskers twitch; she
breathes deeply; she turns her fine, pointed nose about;
she takes up again the task of survival. At the point of
questioning the quality of life she returns to its economics.

NOVEMBER

The coming of November is the time of change for the seals of the Pribilof Islands. For the silver pups it is the end of loafing on soft grass, and rolling deliciously in sand, and splashing in wet pools. It is the shock of finding that mother has not returned. For the older seals it is again the time to embark on the grand winter cruise to pastures of the Pacific. By late winter or spring, some seal or other will have dipped into every square mile of ocean from Japan to the Aleutian Islands, and from Canada to northern Mexico. November is the month of the great exodus.

After she left her pup on the last day of October, the Golden Seal struck a course to the southeast. She would have turned back once more to St. Paul had not a small, insidious change in her body pushed her on to warmer seas. On the first of November she swam near the Island of St. George and five days later she passed in the fog within smell of Bogoslof, the fabulous island that has risen and fallen, and risen again, in historic time.

Ten days out of St. Paul, the Golden Seal drifted at night through Unimak Pass, that broad, wild channel of troubled waters through which so many sea animals pass in transit from the Bering Sea to the Pacific. Soon she was 300 miles from her summer home and was caught up in the countercurrent of the Gulf of Alaska, a stream that carried her steadily farther from the lands of the north.

And the new life sparked within her body last July—
what of that? The single cell divided, split in four, in
eight, in sixteen, in finer and finer subdivisions up to the
hundreds, when the action stopped. Was this life so
faintly gleaming soon to disappear? Not at all. It rested in
an upper chamber of the womb as a translucent sphere no
larger than a grain of crystal sand. There it had lain, this
gleaming blastocyst, without motion and without change,
through August, September, and October.

Suddenly in early November it quickens; the cells
resume their splitting; the pearly embryo is prompted to
continue on a course toward the final form: an Alaska seal.
The horn of the uterus enlarges at the site of the blastocyst like a weak spot in a toy balloon. The swelling
grows to a nesting chamber. By mid-November the cluster of cells will be well along on the track toward the
ancient tetrapod, the four-limbed creature that, depend-
ing on its heritage, will be an amphibian, a reptile, a bird,
or a mammal, such as a seal.

Where is the Golden Seal's first-born and how is he
faring? In the days of early November he spends more
time in English Bay. He returns often to Tolstoi but never
finds his mother; his calls are carried away with the wind.
On the abandoned shore he smells few mothers in milk.
In the meanwhile, he has learned to snatch from the waters of the bay, and to squeeze between his teeth in satisfaction, the small creatures that swarm in the shallow

84

lagoons: the pale amphipods no larger than a fingernail, and the ghost-shrimps, and the silvery sandlance fishes.

The short winter days grow gloomier. One quiet evening in a misty drizzle he finds himself beyond sight of land. He does not return but drifts throughout the night. In the morning, he swims slowly in a ragged mob of a thousand seals toward the south, toward the invisible lure that pulls the older and more experienced animals. He is learning a way; he is learning a pattern of a new and other self, the pelagic self into which every little seal must transmute before it can enjoy the food riches of the deep sea. A week later, still swimming south, he sees the retreating shores of the Aleutian Islands.

THE Golden Seal is now in the Gulf of Alaska with three companions, two cows, and a yearling male. They are loosely bound in a feeling of kinship. The male is floating asleep in the posture of a "jug"—an old expression used by sealers of the past. He has turned his left hind flipper forward and pressed it against his front one in an elegant curve like the handle of a jug. The only part of his body that shows above water is a dark elliptical ring that could be taken at a distance for the root of a floating tree. The other seals in the group are basking in the sun, with only nose and flippers in the air. Their wet flippers twist and turn, flashing now black and now blue from the glance of the sky and the sea.

Long months lie ahead when the Golden Seal will rarely see land; when each day will be a lifting of light and each night a dropping of dark, and the near world a rising and falling of liquid clearness, and a pellucid mirror at the level of her sight.

She feeds mostly at night, when the fishes are outlined in greenish luminescence. As she startles her prey, they break into fireworks, and she hunts them down. Each night she must find and swallow four or five pounds of fish or squid, or perhaps a little more now while she is recovering from the four-month drain of nursing.

In the black nights she descends rhythmically to 100, 200, or even 300 feet to find her food. While she never knows the substance of the next meal, her diet is sure to be monotonous when she finds herself traveling in a large school of fish or squid. Herring, an odd salmon now and then, smelts of several kinds, lantern fishes, tomcod, true cod, pollock, rockfish, sandlance, greenlings, flounders and soles and turbots of many kinds, and opalescent squids.

Chase and snatch with sharp-pointed teeth! Don't bother to chew; swallow them undersea when they're small; rise to the air and shake them to bits when they're large. Cough up the big bones and let the small ones ride through the stomach. Sneak up on the dangling legs of a

floating bird now and then, for fun, but beware! Feathers
are rough to digest.

✦✦✦

ON St. Paul Island in November, the snows come
lightly and disappear. Only on the north slope of Polovina
does the white remain. Elsewhere the crystals melt in a
day or two and the yellow grasses shine again. A few seals
will linger on land into December. These are abnormal;
nearly all are barren; they are out of the mainstream of
seal behavior.

In the village, the resident biologist is talking to Old
Nick, a native. The biologist will stay here through the
winter to study the findings of the past summer and to
plan research for the next. His companions have straggled
south with the seals, some to continue their schooling and
some to spend the winter in the Seattle Laboratory. The
biologist loves the winter time on St. Paul Island, for here
he has time to think, and to feel, and to dream, and to talk
to his friends the natives.

Old Nick was born in the nineteenth century of
Aleut-Russian parentage, with a strain of Polynesian
whaler. His father was a sealing foreman in the Russian
regime. In the cozy parlor of Nick's home there stands a
magnificent samovar of burnished copper, once a utility

but now an art piece. An ikon candle burns in a high corner. As Nick talks, he carves on a tusk of walrus ivory.

"We used to carry the seal skins on our backs, and then Mr. Proctor brought some tractors on the ship to carry them. It was awful hard. In those days they just left the seal bodies on the killing fields after they skinned them. Oh, the flies! The flies were so bad that the sunny side of Government House was all black. Mr. Johnston—he was the superintendent later—was walking home from Zapadni one evening and it got dark and he was barefooted—he liked to take off his shoes, said it made his feet strong—and he was walking in those old wagon ruts and he felt a funny feeling in his toes and he looked down and he was walking on a pile of fly worms that had fallen into the ruts and couldn't get out—millions and millions.

"We used to drive bull sea lions nine miles, from Northeast Point to the village. We made them carry their own skins to where we could take them for *bidarras*. Nowadays we cover these boats with canvas instead of skins. It took us three weeks in dry weather. We would scare them along by clapping sticks and waving flags or umbrellas."

The biologist has an inspiration. "Nick," he says, "would it be possible for you to butcher a seal for me the way the old people did when they lived on seal meat? Could you tell me the names of the parts and which parts you ate?"

Nick agrees. The biologist removes a frozen carcass from the locker and by morning it is thawed. He lays down a white sheet and asks Nick to place upon it the dissected bits, but Nick can't remember all the old names, so he calls for help from Feodor and Dorofy, who are spitting away their retirement years near the stove of the carpenter shop.

"This is the *kalex*," says Feodor, pointing to the brain. "The shoulder is the *chuyux*. All this is the *saxo-yin*"; he indicates the trunk, ribs, and backbone. The biologist recognizes some of the names as Aleut, others as Russian derivatives. Nick's word for the leathery hind flipper, *preschatka,* is surely the Russian diminutive for glove.

The biologist arranges the parts in a neat pattern, as a draftsman would lay out an exploded diagram, and photographs the ensemble for his historical record.

"You've got the ears there. One time my father cut off a hundred pairs of ears." The biologist looks blank. "The Russians wanted to find out if the bachelors would come back to the same place. They cut off the ears at Lukanin and sure enough the seals came back next year."

Old Ivan has appeared in the meantime with the hope that he can tell *his* stories. There is time for only one.

"I think about this because the fog is here today," he says. "When I was a little kid, I walked out to Marunich all by myself, and then the fog came. At night the fog went away. I was awful cold, and I saw lights moving around on the ground and I was scared it was the bad people. I hid in the grass. But next day I found it was only my folks with lanterns looking for me."

DECEMBER

The ocean pathways followed by the seals in December are not well known, for the ocean is very large and the seals are very small. Men predict where seals will be found in December but only estimate the routes they will take to get there. Old charts showing their regular courses were largely guesswork and were biased by a feeling that American seals and Asian seals should have no truck with one another in winter or in any other season.

Be that as it may, the fat harem bull who mated with the Golden Seal in July is now in the shelter of the Shumagin Islands of Alaska, at Latitude 55 North. Here he will stay through winter and spring. Many of his companion males of breeding age will also remain in Alaskan waters. They are few in number, for out of a hundred born only three or four survive the hazards of the sealing drives and the perils of nature to reach age ten, the average age of a harem bull.

Food is plentiful the year around in the Shumagins, the great size of the bull's body helps to keep him warm, and the farther north he stays in winter, the better will be his chances of returning early to the breeding ground in spring and of staking out a choice territory. These are reasonable answers to the question: why don't the bulls go south in winter with the cows and pups?

Here in the Shumagins the harem bull feeds nightly

in shallow, rich waters, threading his way through tearing reefs and weedy passages that a sober fisherman would shun. On the east side of his feeding range he stares at the shining landmark of Veniaminof and on the west Pavlof —the pure white volcanoes that stand 8,000 feet above the sea. From the tip of each lofty peak a white cloud of steam forever forms and drifts off to a thin, invisible end in the frozen air. The mountains are white down to the water's edge. Their slopes are blue-deathly cold in shadow, and even where the sun illuminates them they gleam coldly.

The pup of the Golden Seal is now feeding in the Inside Passage—the protected steamer route between Puget Sound and Skagway. The passage across the Gulf of Alaska was terrifying. Hardly had he cleared the Aleutian Islands when he was caught up in the great seas of winter on the North Pacific. Day after day and night after night he rode one mountainous wave after another. He rode the tops that sheared away in the wind and let him down, dizzy and confused, in the green troughs. He swirled and tumbled with no sense of direction. Familiar land was gone beyond sight and smell. Now and then a majestic sea would lift him high and poise him for a second where he could see across the moving ocean to the skyline. And now and then he would see, in a green submarine blur, the dark shape of another pup—a glimpse, and gone.

He came at last in days without reckoning to a quiet

reach, the Dixon Entrance to British Columbia. At the turn of Kaigani Point he felt the slackening of the surging forces that had torn and worried his small body for three weeks. Suddenly the sea was calm. He drifted like a dead thing for six hours, holding his buoyancy at the top by deep reflexes that would never quite let his lungs expel all their volume of air. Today he woke, ravenously hungry and now he is exploring the briny delights of the Inside Passage.

He is very thin. When he left Tolstoi in November he weighed 35 pounds; now in December he is down to 28. Happily he is near the turning point when his gains will meet his losses—when he will have learned to catch food in proportion to his needs.

The Golden Seal finds her present crossing of the Gulf easier than those of other years. She swims toward the east, and steadily toward the east. She raises land at last near Sitka, the old Russian capital of Alaska, and turns toward the shelter of Crawfish Inlet. Here she sees other pregnant cows and here she lingers through December, feeding on the shoals of fat silver herring that gather in salt water at the mouths of the streams. Only occasionally does she crawl briefly onto the beach; the shadows of the dark spruce forest seem to create a vague apprehension in her, as if they stirred racial memories of predatory wolf and bear and cougar.

On the morning of Christmas Day she is feeding in a small, hidden bay hemmed in by the somber foothills of the coastal range. The hills are streaked with white where old fires and avalanches have cleared away the timber, opening the snowfields to the sky. The tide at the moment is low-water slack; the round boulders of the rocky shore drip with pungent weeds waiting the return of the sea. Three scoters shoot like arrows on whistling wings above her head, bound on some errand of great demand up the bay.

On the eastern shore a wisp of blue smoke began to rise last evening and is still rising, mingling with the little fog-clouds that form and dissolve above the bay. A light, cool breeze riffles the water. In the direction of the smoke, a dugout canoe now appears as a gray form growing ever larger. Slowly the Golden Seal moves away, leaving two companions asleep on the surface, glutted with herring and at peace with the world. The lapping of delicate waves against the canoe and the drip of the paddle are lost in the sigh of the morning breeze. A bald eagle watches quietly from a hillside.

The Indian sealer in the canoe rests his paddle on the thwarts and lets the canoe glide, quartering along the breeze, on a course which brings it 30 feet from the seals. He crouches, fails to control a quick sucking of breath, and in the same breath hurls a spear. The animals dive, but as the rump of one rises, a steel point punctures her skin and lodges deep within the muscles. The water explodes. The man sees the 8-foot shaft of his weapon floating on the surface and he sees that the point is gone; he smiles. The seal rises 50 feet away, struggling against a stout line that runs from the spear point to the canoe. For ten minutes the man plays his catch, trembling with fatigue, for he is an old man. When the line slackens, he pulls, and when it tightens, he holds his craft against the jerking of the victim. The seal is finally alongside the canoe and he swings a wooden club. As he pulls the dripping creature aboard she gasps in blind fury and bites the blade of his paddle, tearing out splinters.

The old man is the last of the Sitka sealers. The young men no longer care to exercise their legal right to take seals by primitive methods. Once in a while one will go down to Crawfish Inlet with a news photographer in a clumsy, half-humorous effort to reconstruct for him the ancient ways of the Tlingits. Soon, though, their sealing spears will be rotted away or sold to museums, and there will be only the legal privilege, spelled out in the fine print of the Fur Seal Treaty.

Back in camp, the old man skins the seal and salts down the pelt beneath a rain-shelter of split-cedar boards. He stokes the fire, and as he fries a slab of liver for his breakfast, he puffs on an ancient pipe. His beautiful brown face settles into a map of seamy content, wrinkle upon wrinkle, while his dark eyes glow with ancient memories in the light of the fire.

As December draws to an end, squalls of hissing sleet come daily to Crawfish Inlet, and the Golden Seal turns south. Swimming and feeding, boosted by the flow of the North Pacific Drift, she follows the edge of the continental shelf, and by early January has passed beyond the Queen Charlotte Islands to the tip of Vancouver Island.

✦˙✦
✦ ✦ ✦

ONE of the biologists has settled for the winter in the Seattle Laboratory, a center of inquiry into the biology of seals, whales and porpoises, sea cows, and sea otters—the marine mammals of all the seas. Though this laboratory is not widely known, it is a jewel of its kind, a small repository of information and expertise. Here he will work until spring, when again he will fly to Alaska to meet the incoming seals. Now he studies the frozen, and dried, and pickled remains of seals collected during the recent summer.

"Where," he asks, "are the blood vessels of the flippers, and knowing where they run, where should we clip our metal tags in order to miss them?" Photographs by X ray are called for. "When do the teeth of the fetal seal begin to form, and what, if any, are the implications for management of the seals?" Perhaps the development of the teeth in pups found dead on the beach will give a clue to the time and cause of death. "When does the yearly change of fur and hair take place? What stimulates the change? Is it the shortening length of daylight in July and August, or is it some other peculiar thrust of the environment, or some rhythmic movement within the body, that initiates the molt?"

Then he turns to a broader question, a question that is often asked but never answered: How shall the Fur Seal Islands be managed for the greatest long-time good of man? It is a question of land-use policy, or land-use ethic. It is the kind of question that nowadays is being asked with increasing urgency by private as well as public planners.

With respect to the Fur Seal Islands, a recurrent question is: How intensively should the landscape and the wildlife resources in seals, foxes, birds, and other species be "managed" or "developed" there?

At one extreme, the biologist foresees the growth of a commercial atmosphere. St. Paul village will have a harbor protected by an artificial breakwater. Fishing vessels will come and go, contributing to the economy of the natives. Because the skins of the foxes are of mediocre quality and bring little revenue, the stock will be poisoned off. Because the sea lions compete with the fur seals for fish, and themselves are of little value, they too will be "controlled"—a government euphemism for "shot." Because the tourist trade in summer is growing, the landscape will be decorated by the introduction of foreign wildlife species, such as musk-oxen from the mainland. These possibilities are not imaginary; they are real—the biologist has heard them talked about in government circles.

He recalls the history of the reindeer transplanted to the Pribilofs from Siberian stock. They survived on one island for forty years, then disappeared. On another island they survived for fifteen years, then suddenly exploded to a population of over two thousand. Deer invaded the village streets; they grazed in the cemetery and along the seal rookeries. More quickly than they had multiplied, they died away; the last one of the brood was seen in 1951. New stock was replanted that same year.

The biologist is opposed to transplanting wild animals unless to fill a void, and then only with species that will fit into the new environment. Throughout history, men have tried to play God by moving rabbits, goats, sparrows, mongooses, and a hundred other species to oceanic islands and island continents, and later have wished to God they hadn't.

✦✦✦

WHILE the Golden Seal's pup feeds in the shelter of the Queen Charlotte Islands in late December, hundreds of his class mates are dying on the open sea. This is nature's way of rejecting the unfit; the individual is sacrificed for the species.

All little seals obey a law of the open sea: that a warm-blooded mammal must be of a certain size in order to survive. The Alaska fur-seal pup at the low point of its briny career in midwinter is the smallest deep-sea mammal in the world. In January–February the female is down to about 18 pounds, the male to about 22 pounds.

So, hundreds of the class mates of the Golden Seal's

pup are dying. Many of the wasted bodies disappear without trace, torn by sharks and other large fishes and later reduced to molecules by the action of smaller fishes and squids, swimming crabs and mollusks, plankton animals, and finally molds and bacteria. Some of the bodies balloon with gases and sail to the shores of Washington and Oregon, where they lodge among the drift. Here they are found by beachcombers scouring the coast for agates, glass balls, useful planks of teak and mahogany, Japanese tea cartons, and polished roots and branches gnarled and twisted like ancient hands. The bodies of the seals may weigh no more than they did at birth six months earlier; they can be held suspended between one's thumb and forefinger.

When the Golden Seal reached the tip of Vancouver Island she was about to continue south in the lee of the island; then she struck an offensive current reeking of sulfur—a stream of bitter wastes discharged from a pulp mill somewhere out of sight. She veered to the west and struck for the blue water of the sea outside the continental shelf, 20 miles from land. Here, beyond the influence of the coastal streams, some of them turbid with gray glacial mud and others tainted with the garbage of civilization, she now feeds contentedly. Off to the east she sees a line of puffy clouds that marks the outer boundary of the shelf, where warm air rising from the water of the shelf meets the chill air of the deep sea.

Shortly after sunset at 4:30, she begins to dive rhythmically to shallow depths between 10 and 100 feet, and as she hunts for fish and squid, many of the prey species are rising to the upper layers in pursuit of *their* prey: the dwarf crustaceans, rotifers, transparent mollusks, arrow worms, and floating larvae of barnacles, sea snails, clams, and starfishes. She moves without effort, rotating slowly in the dim translucence, now on her back and now on her belly. Even by starlight she sees the dark silhouettes of the fish above her head and seizes them in a surge of power.

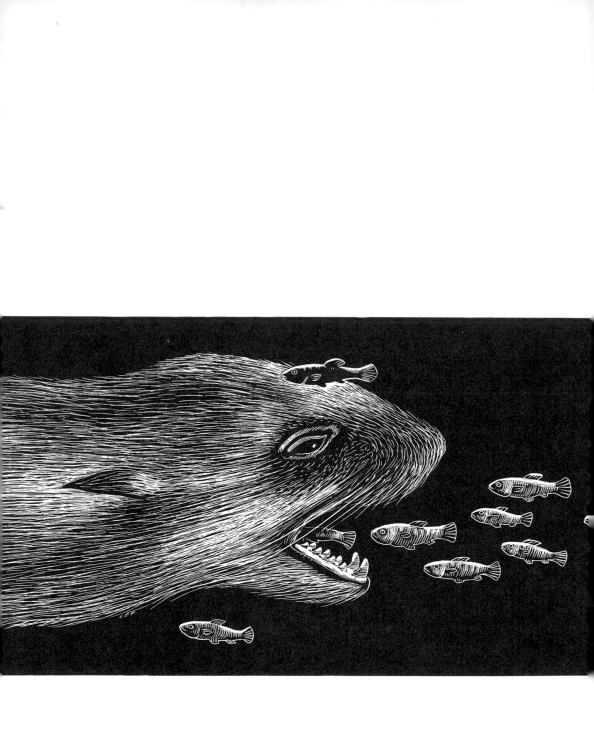

JANUARY

In their clumsy words men try to say what they feel about the world ocean. They try to describe the indescribable, and with the noblest of phrases they fall short. The ocean rolls on, untouched by words. It rolls to the turning of the earth, and the heat and pull of the sun, and the drag of the moon, and the influences of all the solid and gaseous matter in the universe. The deep and dark blue ocean penetrates in time the smallest crannies of the caves of earth and sucks out slowly the chemical ions of the old earth-rock, wafts them away in salty streams, and drops them in gray-purple oozes on its bed, where they lie softly stirring for a thousand years until other layers of ooze press them down, and they subside into soft rock— and in a hundred million years into stone.

The Golden Seal's pup, now considered a yearling, continues to feed in the labyrinthine passages of the lee side of the Queen Charlotte Islands until spring. Then he is taken up in the Alaska Current and carried in a great cyclonic eddy out to sea. Only once in the next year and a half will he enter the realms of man, when a sailor looking down from the deck of a Coast Guard weather ship north of the Hawaiian Islands will spy a dark speck upon the ocean plain. The sailor will train his glass upon it and will write a few words in the log under "Birds and

Animals Sighted." The ship will throb ahead on her lonely course, 10 miles to a leg, squaring a circle around an invisible fix, day and night and week after week. Not until he is fourteen months old, in September of his second year, will the pup return to Tolstoi rookery.

The fetus in the womb of the Golden Seal is beginning to gather momentum on its way to a rendezvous with life or death on the wet rocks of Tolstoi next July. It is a pink animalcule the size of a man's thumb, an ounce in weight, smooth of surface except for the snout, where twenty-four whiskers have erupted through the translucent skin. Why are the whiskers called so soon into being? The fetus has yet to grow more than a hundredfold in size; there is ample time, one would think, for the bristles to materialize—yet here they are. Their early coming suggests that they will later have complex roles to play in sensory orientation, in sex display, in food gathering, and in grooming of the body.

The Golden Seal swims lazily through the waters along Vancouver Island on a course that brings her at times over the continental shelf and at times a hundred miles beyond it. On the twelfth of January she crosses the invisible line traveled by the deepwater vessels from Seattle to Yokohama—4,254 weary miles from port to port.

She daily finds herself feeding side by side with dolphins, the splendid playboys of the sea. They have no effect on her behavior nor she on theirs; the languages of the two species are very different. Often in the cool green depths they overtake her and shoot beyond, leaving quick images of planes and angles, thrust and flare of burnished flanks. She cannot match their speed or their careless manner of seizing fish after fish in rushing flight.

It would not be true to say that she feeds on all forms of life, but she does take at least a hundred kinds of prey. Small silvery fishes, like anchovy, herring, and saury, that travel in schools of millions are the mainstay of her diet. The schools are not continuous; she hunts them down by all the clues they give: the bright flash of countless bodies turning as one, the cripples that fall behind and mark the trail, and the fishy juices that linger long and impinge upon her tongue.

Some of the fishes in her diet are larger ones. These she kills or wounds, one at a time, with thirty-six teeth, all sharply pointed, which interlock to form a trap from which not even a minnow can escape. The rockfishes are bass-like, big of mouth, and painted with varicolored hues and patterns. Fishermen take them by the millions of pounds from British Columbia waters alone, and the Golden Seal takes her own and unreported share. She takes the four species of salmon when they are small enough to handle. A chinook may reach a weight of more than 100 pounds. She often takes the sablefish, a stream-lined fish containing, in spring, tasty masses of spawn. One kind she pursues with caution and only when she is hungry: the ratfish, so called from its chisel teeth. It has a vicious dorsal spine, its flesh is slightly poisonous, and its framework is gristly rather than bony. Fossils of this repulsive creature excavated from rocks 200 million years old resemble living forms.

✦ ✦
✦ ✦

IN the Seattle Laboratory in January a biologist reviews the report of a task force for the study of humane methods of killing seals. This force, or committee, was appointed as a result of criticism that fur seals, in the twentieth century after Christ, were still being killed by clubbing.

The criticism had been engendered by the killing of harp seals on the North Atlantic ice in spring. To most people, a seal is a seal. They do not distinguish between the killing of "whitecoats," or newborn harp seals, on the Atlantic ice and the killing of bachelor fur seals on the Pribilofs. In the harp-seal industry, there have indeed been instances of callousness and cruelty. There have been allegations, too, that certain photographers deliberately staged the skinning of live seals to get sensational pictures. True or false, the publicity once caused the sealskin market to tumble, and members of the Canadian Parliament to argue, and Canadian citizens to write five thousand letters in three days to their government.

It is good, the biologist thinks, to entertain new ideas about the cropping of Alaska fur seals, if for no other reason than to challenge the managing agency. Government bureaus tend to become set in their ways, to respect increasingly their own wisdom and authority.

So the task force visited St. Paul Island. It tested various ways of killing seals: suffocating them in carbon dioxide, and electrocuting them, and shooting them with bullets and with captive bolts—ram-projectiles that travel a few inches from the muzzle of the gun before being halted by a metal ring; these must be held against the head of the victim. All these tools are standard in livestock slaughterhouses, but they were impracticable on the killing fields of St. Paul. Either the seals died slowly and in distress or the men were endangered by their own weapons. Immobilizing drugs had been ruled out at the start because the residues might make the seal meat unfit for use as animal feed.

The task force carried out its assignment fairly, but it could recommend no quicker, cleaner method of killing a seal than bashing in its skull with a heavy club. Questions rose, during the study, of how future investigators could measure sensitivity to pain and clock the exact times of unconsciousness and death. These questions are not as simple as they seem. They also worry human doctors, who ask themselves: How much of human pain is real and how much imaginary—independent of or dependent on the victim's mind?

Not mentioned in the study was the prickly question of how the fur-seal herd can be kept at the level of maximum yield without bringing about the death of pups through starvation. Maximum yield calls for the killing of females, and often a mother will be knocked down before the clubber realizes that she is in milk. Her pup on the rookery will die unless it succeeds in finding a foster mother that has recently lost *her* pup, and from all evidence the chance of a pup's being thus adopted is very slim. In olden times, the sealers on land and sea would justify the killing of females by asserting that "cows all suckle pups not their own," or words to that effect. In a recent decade, 250,000 females of breeding age were killed on the Pribilofs. Happily, that stage of intensive fur-seal management is over; the comparable kill now is fewer than 300 a year.

The biologist lays down the report and thinks, Where do we go from here? Perhaps the option is to continue clubbing seals until public opinion calls for a halt, if it ever does. He wonders, though, Is death any pleasanter by natural starvation, trampling, or disease than by a quick blow on the head? He thinks with pride of man's progress toward a fellow feeling with animals in one generation, since the day when the fish warden of Oregon boasted of killing harbor seals at Tilamook Bay. His method was to fill quart jars with explosives and place them "at spots on the sandy beach where the seals are accustomed to congregate to sun themselves and to mate. [Afterward] the seal-hunters and small boys rush out to dispatch as humanely and effectively as possible the maimed salmon-eaters." And a fisheries engineer of British Columbia told of his success in dynamiting seals on the delta of the

JANUARY

Fraser River. "The explosion [was] more destructive than I had intended. Evidently many of the seals were lying immediately over some of the mines, as their bodies were blown to atoms, not a piece larger than two inches square being found. . . . I am confident that practically every seal within the effective radius of the explosion, both in and out of the water, was killed." All at a cost of only one hundred and fifty dollars for the lot, he bragged.

✦✦✦

IN the last days of January the Golden Seal and four companions of the night are floating lightly on a gentle sea beyond sight of San Francisco Bay. The sun has set. A red, distorted moon works its way through city smoke and emerges from the sea, growing cleaner and whiter as it climbs. Around the bodies of the seals the water is printed with the froth of the air they expire as they hang weightless, with their heads below the surface, listening, forever listening, even in sleep.

The Golden Seal lifts her dripping muzzle and catches the full view of the moon. She empties her lungs in a burbling sigh; her nostrils close; she is gone. Fully rested from her evening nap she dives deeper and deeper in undulating grace as though hunting for pleasure as well as food. Pale bubbles trail from her fur as the pressure deepens. Her flexible rib cage and her windpipe shrink in volume; her lungs collapse; her heartbeat falls to twelve per minute. In six minutes at the most, before she emerges, she will search the cool waters for half a mile.

A black torpedo shoots past her head and, though she has not seen this form of life for a year, she knows it instantly as food. Explosion of vibration without sound . . .bursting ribbon of luminescent green. . . hunter and hunted. The moving play is over in twenty seconds. She rises to the air, crushing a 3-pound silver mackerel. This is all she will eat for a while, so she plays with the body at the surface, stripping bits of metallic skin, separating the bones and diving to recover fragments, until the moon is high in the California heavens.

FEBRUARY

Herring, capelin, squid, and pollock; pollock, squid, capelin, and herring—a rich though monotonous fare now nourishes the bull who bred the Golden Seal last July. In his winter quarters among the Shumagin Islands he has gained 60 pounds since the day when he shuffled down from Tolstoi, gaunt, scarred, dirty of jacket, and foul of breath. His testes are shrunken. It will be two months before he is moved to return to the breeding ground. In good weather he swims 30 miles from the islands to the 100-fathom line where upwellings of Pacific water concentrate the food. In stormy weather he returns to the north, catching glimpses, one by one, of the low peaks that mark the horizon like the teeth of a saw, their valleys carved by water and ice. All the land is white. The breath of the February wind blows steadily near the freezing point, cold and damp, though lacking the cruel bite of continental air.

Popof Island and Pirate Cove, Point Welcome and Wooly Head—he knows them all. In the waters around Simeonof Island he sees each winter the sea otters, the mild, brown dwellers of the kelp whose ancestors were hunted down as intensively as were their mild, brown companions, the tragic Aleut people. A few hundred otters escaped to perpetuate their furry kind. The last full-blooded Aleut died in the 1930s, or so the anthropologists believe.

When his wandering way leads him to the Murie Islets he often lingers for a while in a small and uncharted place of beauty, where a somber forest of seaweed rises in the green underwater of a long ravine between rocks. The stems are rooted in sullen ooze and the glistening trunks lift their upper branches to a shimmer of light. The sapless ribbon-leaves hang as though here they had hung from the beginning. Space and illumination are soft and dilute, without sharpness. All the blacks are greenish brown. The rocky cliffs are perfect in place and form, like the mountains in a Japanese print. They have no substance of their own but glow with the cold apparel of the life that overgrows them altogether. They are an old, encrusted palette upon which an infinite artist is continually changing the colors. Dream world and real world are one, threaded by bubbles that climb softly, each to have its moment in the sun.

Through the quiet of twisting vegetation, small creatures of the sea—a million variations on a theme—wind their aimless ways, or float passively, or flap their filmy wings, or fall twinkling down in deepening gloom to the slime below. Clouds of whirling particles, animated, engage in pinprick love as they drift in slow diffusion through the foliage. From the deepest grottoes, the disembodied eyes of devilfish stare outward through dark and lidded telescopic lenses. Through the corridor the seal moves silently, caught by the illumination and challenged by the weedy pillars through which he must weave his way. His figure is green, barred with quick shadow. He grows smaller in the distance and disappears like unreturning time.

Far to the south and far at sea the Golden Seal is luxuriously following a great school of saury. Lucky indeed she was, off Monterey one night in early February, to hear a sound like rainfall as the sauries skipped from the water and plunged below the surface. For every pound of fish in the air, a hundred pounds were moving below in a vast constellation that seemed to have no leading edge but moved in a steady drift toward the southwest.

The saury is well designed for flying briefly. The fins are set far aft on a slender, foot-long body; the head is sharp and conical. The whole fish, with clean profile and metallic blue-green-and-silver skin, might have been designed—though not so well—by an aircraft engineer.

The Golden Seal is moving with the school, feasting by night and resting in brief snatches during the day. When she wakens, she is never uncertain of the direction taken by the school as she slept. She travels in the company of other fur seals and of bottle-nosed dolphins, white-sided dolphins, and striped dolphins. Hundreds of black-legged kittiwakes and glaucous-winged gulls have followed the sauries out from the coast. The birds feed at the center of the school for a while, then fall behind, to rise again with flapping wings, gorged and stupid. They defecate, as though to lighten their load, and beat their way back to the scene of action.

A bull elephant seal, two tons in weight, has strayed from the Mexican Islas los Coronados and now lies asleep at the surface, sated with fish. Toward noon he will turn back to the islands, for his breeding season will soon begin and a stronger magnet now pulls him away from the delights of the open sea. The Golden Seal passes him carefully down wind, smelling and tasting with open mouth the scent of his body.

✦✦✦

IN Tokyo the annual meeting of the North Pacific Fur Seal Commission is getting underway. Delegates from Canada, Japan, the Soviet Union, and the United States have gathered to talk about ways of conserving the seals and in the discussion to weigh the benefits and disadvantages that might result from various conservation practices.

The Japanese delegate raises the perennial question of the impact of seals upon commercial fisheries. The needs of his people for products of the sea are very high, or something over seven million tons a year, worth two billion dollars. "How much," he wants to know, "will a fur seal eat in a day? How much will two million seals eat in a year? What proportion of their food would otherwise go to feed the hundred million people of my homeland?"

The answers are slow in coming. They dribble out through barriers of scientific ignorance, language differences, and national interests, but they satisfy the delegate. The daily intake of a seal in the wild (a 65-pounder) is about 4 pounds of fish and squid, or 2,500 calories. The intake of all fur seals of all ages in the North Pacific, or 1.7 million animals, approaches a million tons of fish and squid a year.

The last question of the delegate from Japan, touching on the competition between seals and man for the same food, is one that probably will never be answered. Seals, and the hundred organisms upon which they feed at one season or another, and at one place or another, are a myriad cast of actors, coming and going on a shifting stage.

A word from the Soviet delegate has a telling effect. On Bering Island, he says, the native people take annually from 20,000 to 100,000 salmon from the Saranna River, which is only 5 miles from the largest seal rookery on the island. Moreover, he says, he once anchored for several hours near the rookery and with a single line caught three-fourths of a barrel of cod.

With various degrees of reluctance the delegates agree that: "With present knowledge of the causes of mortality in salmon, it is not possible to say that there would be more or fewer salmon if there were no fur seals."

Any answer to the final question is complicated by the national origin of the seals themselves—that is to say, "Whose seals are feeding off whose shores?" Evidence that Asian and American seals intermingle at sea in winter and spring was long known in the diplomatic circles of the treaty nations but did not leak down to the fishery biologists. Each nation held its own secrets for future use in bargaining.

Information rolling in each year from fur-seal research is now piling up an impressive body of fact on the intermingling of seals. One-third of the bachelors wintering in waters off Japan are of Pribilof birth. Pups born on Russian islands later appear in small numbers on American islands, and vice versa. They recognize no national boundaries.

This is not to say that the fur seals of American shores are identical with those of the Russian rookeries. Slight differences in oceanic climate and in topography of the breeding grounds have created differences in the movements of the seals and their pattern of distribution on land.

In the summer of 1960 an American biologist was sent to Robben Island, off the coast of Siberia, to study these differences, also to learn how the Soviet Union runs a *zvyerosovkhoz*, a fur-seal collective farm. He was told in advance to "swab the Russians down for ideas." He and his interpreter were the first Americans to land on Robben Island since Leonhard Stejneger, zoologist of the Smithsonian Institution, in 1896. After many yards of red tape had been cut, they left Japan on a Russian freighter, transferred to another one near Vladivostok, and reached Robben Island in late summer, after the seal-killing season had ended.

Robben Island is a low, grassy rock one-third of a mile long, the summer home of 150,000 seals. The buildings that house the workmen huddle at the base of a plateau covered with nesting murres. Day and night the biologists heard the querulous voices of the adult birds, broken by the cries of nestlings that had tumbled from the rocks and were fumbling in the dim crawl-space beneath their bedroom.

At a place where the bachelor seals can be rounded up during the sealing season, the beach is narrow. The workmen cannot easily surround the animals to cut them off from the sea, so they crawl on hands and knees on the floor of a long sandy tunnel underneath the seals and pop up through a trap door at the water's edge.

The biologist saw the remains of another Soviet invention which was less successful—in fact, it was a flop. It was a giant sieve, or screen, with a wooden grating designed to sort the seals by size as they scrambled along its passageway, prodded from the rear by workmen. It must have been designed by an efficiency expert who had never seen a frightened seal in action or been told that a seal in such a state is a very uncooperative animal indeed.

The biologist enjoyed long talks with the leading fur-seal expert of the Soviet Union, Dr. S.V. Dorofeev. He had lived as a youth with an aunt who danced in the Bolshoi

Ballet. Some day, he said, he would tell how he escaped the purge of intellectuals during the Revolution, but in 1962 he dropped dead during a fur-seal conference in Seattle.

✦✦
✦✦✦

IN late February, the Golden Seal reaches the turn-about point of her migratory path, 300 miles at sea from Monterey, on Latitude 35 North. The older cows, a few of them over twenty years of age, will continue south to the lonely latitudes of Mexico before they feel the urge to return. Someday, the Golden Seal herself will follow the elders of the herd toward the south.

Today she watches the play of four young seals swimming in a line, rising and falling like water serpents. They pass her in a wide circle and return to rest, then race off again in a flash. A three-year cow floats with hissing breath, pushes off with a single stroke of an arm. Her hind flippers sway like the tail of a fish in a loose but powerful rhythm, her body starts to glide ahead, both arms rise in full strength and smash against her sides. She is off at 15 miles an hour, leaving a wake of bubbles, trailing her hind quarters as a stabilizer. She gives a yelp of excitement even before she rises to the surface. The game of follow-the-leader continues until the youngest players tire.

Now the Golden Seal again takes up the search for

food. For an instant she is a dark swan with slender neck leading a larger body, wings outspread in flat planes of power. As she glides ahead in a single pulse her body overtakes her neck. The skin of her back slides away in rippling waves and disappears from her flanks.

She is fast indeed, though she will never catch the master swimmers of the sea, the swordfish and sailfish, the yellowfin and wahoo, when these great silvery creatures race at full speed near 40 miles an hour. The upper limits of speed of the oceanic fishes are still not definitely known, for men have not found a way to measure their explosive rush. (Can it be as great as the speed of a man-made fish of solid lead, dropping through the water at 115 miles an hour? Surely not.)

For no apparent reason—perhaps alerted by a distant crackle of thunder or the sound of a jet plane passing twenty miles away—the Golden Seal rises in the water and stares around the compass. Droplets run in silver beads from the tips of her whiskers; her nostrils flare. Satisfied, she settles back and lets the sun play on her black flippers. Again the sound—and now she sees a swimming creature barely awash. She drops without sound for a closer look. The pupils of her eyes dilate, and she observes the ghostly, greenish belly of a sea turtle. Its head, with cold reptilian stare and tight, determined mouth, leads the way. Its scaly flattened arms beat in regular breast strokes as it moves along in search of drifting seaweed, or in search of something that only a turtle could want. The Golden Seal has never seen this kind of life. She exists today because her ancestors for a million generations learned to beware of strangers, so she makes no move, and the creature disappears.

She has cruised in a wide circle, and as the last light fades from the sky she finds herself again where the four young seals were playing at noon. Suddenly she strikes a water-mass suffused with the blood of her own species— a familiar substance, though unexpected here. She reads no important message in the ruddy stain through which she swims for a full minute, nosing aside odd fragments of flesh and bits of leathery flipper sinking slowly in the dark. All is quiet. She passes on to a cleaner sea. Had she followed this course twenty minutes earlier, the year of the Golden Seal would have ended as sharply as did the lives of those seals who were surprised here by a great white shark.

Twenty-two feet long he was, from pointed snout to sickle tail. His graceful body, slaty gray above and dirty white below, a killing machine perfected during 300 million years of time, melted into the dim water. He slid toward the first seal in awful silence, without ripple or warning, and as he twisted for the kill the circle of his open jaws was as great as the circle of a man's arms. Fifty teeth, two inches long, jagged, knife-like, incredibly beautiful in their functional design, flared whitely in the final instant, then the seal was gone. With an easy roll of its boneless body the shark turned to the second seal, and it too he swallowed whole. The third and fourth victims were seized from behind as they rushed away in fright, side by side, from the scene of the attack. Paralyzed with shock, they felt no pain as the great fish neatly severed their hind flippers in one rush and tore their bodies in the next.

When the Golden Seal went by a hundred yards away, the shark was resting, drenched in the odors and tastes of his kill and unaware of her passing. He was alone, having left the winter feeding grounds of his kind farther off to the south and west, in warmer and deeper waters. He had learned to prey upon the seals and sea lions that frequent the Monterey coast.

FAR to the north, on St. Paul Island, an old man wakes in the night. Some thin, transparent cord, some tiny thread, between his inner self and the outer world is vibrating. He rises and shuffles to the window, thoughtfully scratching his bony chest. That's it—the quiet! The murmur of the sea is stilled; the crashing of the surf on Tolstoi Head has died away. Suspecting the reason, he downs a quick breakfast of porridge, wraps himself in a warm parka, and steps into a flawless dawn. From Zoltoi Sands to the far horizon the Bering Sea is a purple plain of ice, broken and drifting, moving slowly southward. Now the children begin to appear, for they too feel the electric touch of the new weather brought by the coming of the ice. As he has done for eighty years, the old man watches the separate floes as they catch on hidden rocks and sway and turn in quiet circles until they bump along again in the grand parade.

His mind flashes back to the story told by his father's father of the great summer ice of 1836 when the seals and the people died so terribly. The winter had been colder (the grandfather said) than ever before in memory. Many Pribilof Islanders died, for at that time they lived in miserable dugouts in the ground with little more than their own body heat for warmth. When spring came, the sea ice held along the shore as a white wall 20 feet above the surf, and when the pregnant seals came back from migration, only a few succeeded in finding a way through the wall. The others gave birth on narrow beaches where they were beaten by salt spray and where they watched their newborn young disappear with the tides. Four years later, a skeleton class of bachelor seals returned to the ancient hauling grounds of St. Paul.

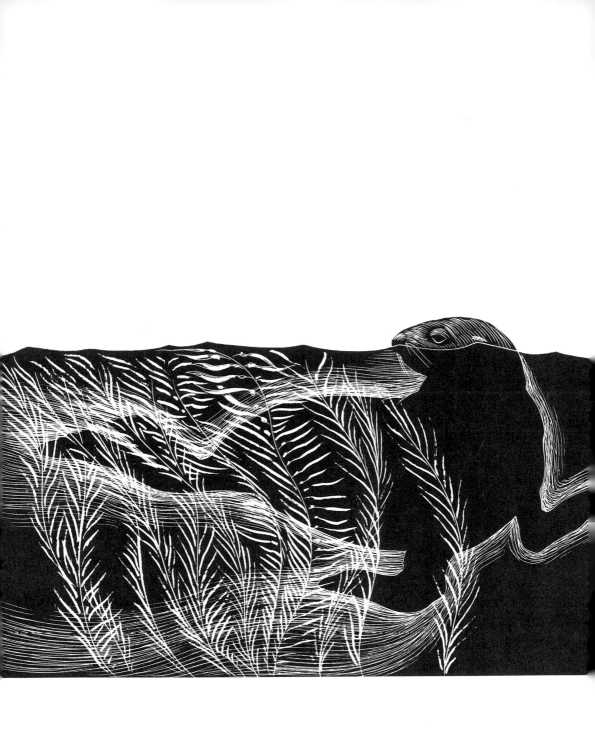

MARCH

Now it is March, and the Golden Seal is idling through a field of floating kelp 70 miles outside the Golden Gate. The stems and leaves of the weed, though detached from their holdfasts on the ocean floor, will stay alive for weeks. At last they will succumb to sunburn, and the collapse of their floats, and the gnawing of tiny mouth-parts, and disease. They will sink in slimy ropes to the deep, where nature will loosen their membranes and take their cells apart, and recycle their atoms in new generations of life.

The brown-and-yellow raft of weed is a glorious playground for two young sea lions who are slopping and slithering through its tangle. They are 300 miles from home, but there is little action at home in March, and, besides, they are too young to be concerned with the upcoming breeding season. Here in the thicket of weed they find small fishes and crabs, and pink swarming shrimps. They are free for a time from the pestering of older relatives. When they tire of chasing one another they sprawl on the kelpy mattress undulating in the swell and breathe weedy, pungent airs like those of their California home.

The Golden Seal watches them in the glow of a bright fog that illuminates the tiniest leaf and stem, the smallest feather dropped from the breast of a passing bird. There are no shadows, and no sounds except the

127

occasional plop of a sculpin leaping from a clearing in the weed.

When she begins to sense a change in the scene she drops her head in the water and listens intently. The low throbbing of a motorship comes from the east. It grows in volume and she turns toward the west. Voices speak out of the fog.

Bam! Bam! She feels a pain like a twisted nerve in her left hind foot. As she bolts in panic she finds herself in the open, with the blue sky overhead and the bright sun streaming down. The prow of an 80-foot seiner breaks the wall of fog, and she sees two men on the peak; they hold shotguns leveled in her direction. Again, *Bam! Bam!* She feels the slam of twenty-four No. 00 magnum slugs in the water above her head, but by now she is 4 feet down and is stroking furiously toward the fog bank. She passes underneath the ship and rises, puffing heavily, in the center of the kelp. A trickle of blood from the leathery web of her flipper is beginning to clot. She will carry for life a neat round hole the size of a pencil as a result of her encounter with a pelagic sealing vessel, but deeper than the wound in her flesh will be the scar on her memory. Never again will she linger within sound or sight of a ship.

✦✦✦

THE seiner that gave the Golden Seal the fright of her life was the *Anna B,* under contract to collect fur seals for biological study by scientists of the United States Government. While she is operating off the California coast, other vessels are collecting seals for the scientists of Canada, Japan, and the Soviet Union.

After the Golden Seal vanishes in the fog, the vessel plows ahead, with the morning sun astern. The captain stands outside the wheelhouse in full control of the engine and the rudder. He sees a dark thing on the glittering sea that could be another seal, or a floating log. He steers toward it, gauges the wind, and cuts the motor. For several minutes the ship glides silently ahead. The hunters at the bow, the deck hands, the engineers, and the cook are motionless. They know the meaning of the moment: prey is being stalked. The ship is barely under way as she nears the object, now identified as two seals sleeping side by side, their flippers touching. At a whispered note of command, the hunters fire as one, and the seals drop their heads in shock. The ship comes to life. Men run to the rail and gaff the bodies with long hooks, haul them to the afterdeck, and signal to the captain to carry on the hunt. One of the seals is dead; the other dies while a biologist ties a label to its flipper. At the instant of death, the reflective membrane of the retina of its eye throws back the flashing yellow of the sun.

Aboard the *Anna B*, the biologist weighs and measures each seal, looks carefully at the flippers for metal tags, cuts off a pair of teeth for estimation of age, and opens the belly to remove the stomach and the reproductive tract.

He draws a blood sample and freezes it to be studied later by a Japanese specialist who has hit upon a novel method of identifying the birthplace of a seal, whether Asian or American. He can distinguish four blood types, and he finds that the percentage of each type varies with the breeding stock, or subpopulation. Though all North Pacific seals look alike, they return to different breeding grounds and are therefore governed by slightly different factors in their blood—cryptic factors, to be sure, but measurable by delicate methods.

With sharp tweezers the biologist picks an assortment of parasitic worms from the carcass and drops them into alcohol for later study. There is still a great mystery about the complex relationship between a seal and the dozen kinds of worms that live within its warm body.

As he opens the second seal he calls in excitement, "Hey, Cliff, twins!" And, indeed, two little fetuses are lying on the deck. They are curled in an arc in the attitudes of the see-no-evil, hear-no-evil monkeys of the Orient, one with a pink flipper over an eye and one with a flipper over an ear. At the halfway mark in their gestation period—four months after implantation, and four months before birth—they are miniature fur seals, weighing only 2 pounds and clothed in delicate gray fuzz.

The biologists are pleased to have the rare specimens. Only fourteen in a thousand pregnancies result in twin embryos, and even fewer in twin births. Though no one knows, the demands on the mother's body may make it impossible for her to rear two pups successfully to the weaning stage in autumn. Some biologists believe, moreover, that the social relationship—one mother, one pup—is so automatic and so firmly fixed in the nursing routine of the seal, that it cannot be broken even when two embryos develop to the time of birth. Fur seals, in adopting the habits that have enabled them to live gracefully in two worlds, aquatic and terrestrial, have dug for themselves a deep evolutionary groove out of which it is increasingly impossible for them to climb.

The *Anna B* is cruising today off the Golden Gate because of the Fur Seal Treaty of 1957 and because of certain reasons for studying seals.

By mutual agreement of the treaty nations, the bloodline of *Callorhinus* must not be allowed to break. Fur seals in token numbers, at least, must be preserved forever. Unless for compelling reasons, men do not have the right to make decisions which future men cannot reverse.

Beyond this ethical consideration, the aim of fur-seal research is to offer guidance to the officials who must make the final, tough decisions on fur-seal population control. These men must compromise a public demand for large herds, which will produce the greatest revenue, and one for small herds, which will inflict the least damage upon the fishing industry. The voice of the biologist unfortunately is weak and in the final conference is often lost in the clamor of the officials and the politicians. The tragedy of world whaling is a case in point.

Given the challenge, though, the fur biologists do their best to find out, through research on the high seas, certain facts that they cannot obtain on the breeding grounds. Seals are more evenly distributed by age and sex while they are at sea and thus are a better source of random samples. The pregnancy rate, for example, is misleadingly high on land; a maternity ward is not the place to collect data on pregnancy rates!

The food habits of the seals are best learned at sea, for on land their stomachs are usually empty. To be sure, roundabout efforts have been made on land to understand their diet through examination of fish earbones recovered from seal "spewings." Each kind of fish has a characteristic earbone, shaped like an artist's easel and sculptured distinctively like a fingerprint. These traces are a poor substitute, though, for the evidence of stomach contents of seals shot in the very act of feeding.

Finally, the seagoing biologist gets insight into the intermingling of Asian and American stocks, and what he learns is useful to the treaty statesmen. Knowing, for example, the numbers of Alaskan and Russian seals that winter off Japan, he can say: "If the Japanese were allowed to take ten thousand of these in their pelagic fishery, it would cut the Alaskan harvest on land by x percent and the Russian harvest on land by y percent." So the statesmen agree that all seals shall be taken on land under strict control and that the profits shall be distributed fairly among the treaty nations.

⁺⁺⁺

AFTER her encounter with the motorship, the Golden Seal moved northward at a lively pace to waters off the forested shores of Eureka, California. Here under the midday sun she now lies belly up with her legs spread, grooming her thick, oily fur. She smooths her face with alternate strokes of her hands. These are flexible, water resistant, and covered on the palm surface with fine treads—perfect squeegees. She somersaults in a weightless wheel and reappears with one hind flipper dressing down the back of her neck. She pauses in "prayer," the tips of her fore flippers together and raised toward the blue vault. She turns her head right and left, keeping one wary eye toward the west where a lumber freighter plows the sea, and the other wary eye toward the east where a small vessel has been fussing near the coast since ten o'clock.

It is hard to say why the Golden Seal is so given to cleaning herself, since she lives in the water day and night. Perhaps the slime of her food penetrates the fur

133

fibers and causes irritation. Perhaps she is annoyed by organisms that settle on her coat in the few places where she cannot reach to scrub. Small patches of algae tinge her body here and there with reddish brown, while goose-neck barnacles hitch-hike on her fur, doomed to die when she hauls out on land in summer.

She slides through the water quietly to approach a sleeping bachelor who carries a strange attachment on his back. It looks like a strand of coarse yellow grass sprouting from a warty scar on the fur, but in fact it is a length of sinew line twisted by the hands of an aborigine far away. Beneath the skin, embedded in the blubber, is the point of a harpoon dissolving in granules of rust. It does not bother the seal. He is young and vigorous and has long forgotten the hot flash of pain that struck him one foggy morning a year ago in Kamchatka Bay.

THE small boat engaged in queer maneuvers off Eureka carries on board two relatives of the Golden Seal, a half-sister and a half-brother of the previous year class on Tolstoi, five years old, going on six. They now have name-tags and have lost their freedom; they have been drafted into the ranks of the experimental animals who work for a comfortable living and a kind word now and then. The seals are called Hydra and King, and they are personnel, in a manner of speaking, of the 40-foot research vessel *Catalyst,* of California Institute. The experiment of the day is concerned with the ability of a seal to perform a task in the free open sea and return on command. Once released, will the animal take off for the wild blue yonder, never to return, or will it remember its carefree days at the Institute?

Hydra will certainly remain loyal, for she was raised from infancy in the world of man and thinks she *is* a man. She is a lucky survivor of an experiment on St. Paul Island. Five years ago, four pups were taken by Caesarian section and were held in the laboratory to be infested with hookworm larvae as part of a study of this deadly parasite. To feed the captives, a biologist brought from the rookery each morning the bulging stomachs of several "tankers" —pups that had just fed naturally before they were humanely killed. He introduced the warm, curdled milk into the throats of the captives by stomach tube. It was a complicated business, though reasonably successful. Hydra and two little males survived the hookworm test; the other pup succumbed. The three survivors developed an immunity to the worm just as they would have in the wild. They became great favorites around the St. Paul laboratory, and with the southward migration of the biologists in autumn, they were flown to California Institute, where they were weaned and placed in the pinniped pool.

During her five years at the Facility, Hydra was carefully trained. One of her assignments was to test a zoo diet known as Vita-Fare, a sort of gray sausage stuffed with fish meal, fish oil, corn, and vitamins. The veterinarians hoped that it would become a standard fare, cheaper, easier to handle, and safer to feed than frozen fish. Though Hydra learned to swallow the stuff, she was never enthusiastic about it. During the test period she was, like Mark Twain's fly that crawled from the inkwell, "alive but discouraged."

One of Hydra's companions eventually ran into trouble. Little Arthur was traded to a city zoo, where he lived happily until September of his third year. For a few days, then, he was off his feed, and one morning was found dead on the bottom of his pool. Upon autopsy, the killer was revealed: copper poisoning. In his stomach there were 321 pennies, 12 nickels, 8 dimes, 1 West German pfennig, a button, a metal washer, and 16 pebbles—3 pounds in all.

The third companion was King, the other trainee now aboard the *Catalyst*. His career paralleled that of Hydra until both were a year old; then King was loaned to a special zoo for training. The aim was not to exploit him for his entertainment value but to measure his learning ability as compared with that of the ordinary "trained seal" of zoos and circuses—the California sea lion. He was put through the same course as a sea lion, and by the same experienced trainer. He learned to shake hands, clap, say his prayers, roll over, balance a ball, and take a shower. The trainer, who had never seen a fur seal in its native habitat, did not realize how incredibly far from the wild state he had brought King along when the animal finally stood on his hands, with feet in the air, and balanced a baton on his upturned nose!

Hydra and King are now resting on the deck of the

Catalyst in a slow swell moving across the sea. They have a simple assignment: to dive to a target and return for a food reward. The biologists are hoping for the payoff of weeks of patient training that will, for the first time, provide data on the maximum depth to which a fur seal will dive and the length of time it will stay under in the free, open sea. The weather holding fair, Hydra is released from her pen at one o'clock. She leaps eagerly from the rail and aquaplanes on the sea, leaving a creamy wake. A biologist lowers a metal box to a measured depth of 50 feet, then activates a circuit. A lamp begins to flash rhythmically on the box, and a buzzer to sound the steady note of middle C. Hydra turns to the source of sight and sound; it is a familiar target. She pulls to a stop without effort and touches a lever protruding from the box. The signals end and are replaced by a new tone an octave higher emanating from a buzzer under the boom of the *Catalyst.* Up she speeds and breaks the surface in the shadow of the hull. The biologist tosses her a fat herring. (Though there are live fish in the sea, she ignores them; she has been dependent upon man too long.) The biologist now lowers the box to 100 feet and Hydra repeats her act. As the sun moves across the sky and the target goes deeper and deeper, Hydra loses interest. At 300 feet the biologist watches her faint image on a telescanner. She coasts toward the box, then veers away and shoots for the surface after a total dive of four and one-half minutes. He coaxes her into a live-well, or floating cage, and the crew hoist her aboard. Now it is King's turn.

There has been some doubt about King's loyalty to science. He has had too many trainers and has changed his allegiance too often. In the freedom of the open sea he will perhaps go AWOL at a loss to the Institute of several thousand dollars, so the biologists have harnessed him with a simple, lightweight device designed to reinforce his patriotism. It is a deflated rubber balloon, with a calcium carbide pill and a slow-dissolving trigger of salt and boric acid.

Away he goes! The buzzer and the light announce their charms in vain. King is wild with excitement. He dives under the keel and surfaces on the other side, then heads for the open sea, leaping clear of the water in spurts, like a watermelon seed popping from pressed fingers. The biologist smiles wryly. "Well, if our calculations are right, old King has another eighty-six minutes of fun." The crew haul in the target, the captain sends a lookout to the crow's nest, and the *Catalyst* throbs away in the direction of the departed guest. King does not avoid the ship, though he often changes course and once he rises in the wake behind it. When the ship is 50 feet from him, the biologist again sounds the food buzzer, but King is having too much fun; he ignores the dinner call. Suddenly he hears a hiss as the balloon fills with acetylene. He tries to dive but can only wallow at the surface. The *Catalyst* comes along side and the crew lift him in a dip net and dump him on the deck. Something has been added to the scenario. He looks at them with what might be a hurt expression, then falls at once into sleep. The *Catalyst* heads for port.

The biologists are tired. They stare at the dismal tangle of gear on the deck and decide to let it lie. With steaming mugs of coffee cradled in their hands they sprawl on the hatch for a while and take up an old discussion. It deals with a question that often hangs in the air, unspoken, while they are handling seals—the question of seal "intelligence." At times, the men will speak directly and bitterly of the "stubbornness" or "stupidity" of a certain one, and, moments later, they will marvel at its quick, graceful movements in the water. They agree that seals are remarkably adept at learning tricks that call for intricate body motions and for a sharp sense of timing and balance. These, however, do not add up to intelligence in the usual sense of the word.

"Ken," inquires one of the men, "you've been making plastic impressions of brain cases. How does a seal compare with a dog for brains?"

"Well, you've got to compare animals of the same size"—he pauses—"I weighed the brain of a bachelor seal at twelve ounces. That is much larger than a dog's brain, maybe twice as large. The weight of the brain is a rough measure of intelligence. A seal's brain is only one-third as heavy as a dolphin's of comparable body size, and dolphins and porpoises are considered to be smart animals."

The first man continues: "The head of a seal pup always seems to be too large for its body. Why so?"

"Well, the brain of a young seal develops more rapidly than the brain of a child, but I'm only saying that the seal is precocious, or, if you wish, that birth in the human species is very premature. The brain of a seal at birth is already half of its adult size; the brain of a man at birth is only one-quarter of the size it will be at, say, age eighteen to twenty years."

The pelagic researcher *Anna B* has meanwhile turned south into Monterey Bay to find a quiet reach where a new kind of test can be made. The question has arisen: How can we capture fur seals alive on the open sea? Though many hundreds of seals have been taken alive for science on the breeding grounds in summer and fall, none has ever been taken at sea in winter and spring. The biologists want to outwit a seal in its watery home where the animal is supremely master of the man. Last winter they tested a floating cage baited with live herring, a device upon which the seals were supposed to climb, then fall through a trapdoor to a tiny prison. A radio beacon marked the course of the cage as it rode for three days in the path of the migrating seals. The gulls soon found it and carelessly limed its surface with white as they rode on its superstructure in the sea winds. A few seals approached it in idle curiosity, and several rubbed their backs against it, but none would venture aboard the wooden frame so clearly alien to the world of a seal.

So, this afternoon, the men of the *Anna B* have set a floating gill-net 200 feet long, from the lower edge of which most of the weights have been removed. Bright orange floats bob at the surface and reveal in sinuous lines the shifting of the tides. The vessel drifts a quarter-mile away. In the last light of evening, two biologists run the

140

trapline in a "quiet boat," a rubber pontoon-catamaran propelled by an electric motor. Two cormorants and a sculpin of some kind, dimly seen in the dusk, are struggling in the surface webbing of the net. The men cut them loose and turn back to the swaying lights of the mother ship.

At daybreak, the ship gets underway and approaches the net, while the biologists eagerly search the water with glasses. The sinuous line is beaded with dark forms, some quiet and others moving. A power dory is lowered and the men retrieve their catch: three young fur seals (fighting mad), another seal drowned with a choking nylon loop around its throat, four cormorants (alive but tattered), assorted fishes, and a frightful mess of green seaweeds and jellyfishes.

Says the leader: "If seals were able to communicate, you'd think that the first one caught would have warned the others. I suppose it was all too complicated for a non-human language."

The men are highly pleased with their success, and only later, on the Coast Guard dock at Monterey, while they work for hours with rubber gloves at cleaning the net of debris, and mending the torn places, do they agree that *surely* there must be an easier way to catch fur seals alive. But theirs is a pioneer achievement. Three healthy seals are now on their way by truck to California Institute, where the physiology of wild seals in the nonbreeding season will soon be under study for the first time.

APRIL

Swimming ever northward, the Golden Seal had crossed the latitude of the boundary line between California and Oregon during the last week of March. As the April sun begins to warm the sea, the immense liquid meadow breaks into bloom. In a matter of days its shimmering surface is streaked with yellow swirls as fertilizing currents rise to the top and conflow. They quicken the cell division of the diatoms. When the Golden Seal floats quietly with open eyes beneath the surface she sees the individual plants as tiny flecks, their glassy capsules twinkling in the filtered sunlight. Though during the winter months it was hard to tell one day from another, now the grand procession of life is again underway and each new morning brings a change of scene. In the spring, as in every spring, the world is reborn.

She continues on her way toward the north and west, retracing her autumn path along the continental slope. Twenty-two hundred miles to go in a hundred days, and the fetus in her womb is beginning to twist and turn. She feeds both by day and by night. Often at night, bathed in the moon's flood, she looks up through the water and sees the white orb jerking in the waves. Often, in the day, a blinding fog steals out from the land and closes off her world. Often she sees an uprooted tree go riding by, with a harbor seal, or a gull, or a flock of arctic terns resting among its branches.

143

On the fifth of April, where the outflow of the great Columbia River pours its waters over Pacific brine, she is attracted by a fishlike animal she has never seen before. A dark brown, naked, slimy cylinder, the size of a broom handle and 2 feet long, wriggles across her vision. She grasps it uncertainly by the middle and finds it a rippling, rubbery mass of muscle. It quickly turns its head and strikes her with a mouth that has no jaws but only a sucking disk lined with rasping teeth. It tries to fasten on her flesh, but her heavy fur protects her from the attacker: a parasitic lamprey. In one firm bite she severs its body and swallows the body parts. These have a delicate oily flavor and contain no bones at all. She searches for others like this tasty fish, but all have moved on toward the continent and toward the rivers where they will spawn.

The chronicle of the Golden Seal in April is rather uneventful. She sees no land, though somewhere off to the east the coastal ranges of Washington and Canada lie green and dripping in the oceanic mists. She swims and feeds. Like any pregnant female, she pauses now and then for a nap. All day today she has followed the lee of a wooden hulk, a bit of wreckage that once was a trolling boat. It is a mournful structure of broken boards and spars and trailing lines. A rising wind from the southeast carries it along at the same pace as the travel of the Golden Seal, and as night falls, she continues to swim or drift in the dark of its reflection. She is aware of the keening of the wind through the wreckage, the sound of the sea, and the brightening radiance of the Milky Way above her.

APRIL

Though her myopic eyes, adjusted to vision undersea, cannot distinguish individual stars, the sweep and timing of the great constellations help to guide her on her migratory course.

The wind picks up and the full orchestra of the ocean begins to play—the drums and reeds, the pipes and strings. She hears the booming swell and slow retreat of each separate wave. She is at the center of an enormous, vibrating fullness of oceanic sound. Her body becomes part of the rhythm, and her throat vibrates in sympathy. All night, while Orion wheels and the flickering stars bathe her in their distant light, she rides the storm beside the frail craft.

Far away, on the thirteenth of April a bull seal pushes his way through floating ice and approaches the beach of Tolstoi. He is the first of his kind, the first arrival of the new year.

Each winter the sea ice is driven by winds and currents from the Arctic Ocean into Bering Sea. By the time it reaches the Pribilofs it is broken and wind-eroded. Crags of white higher than a man's head stand against the dark gray sky. Between the floes, submerged forms of mystery shine through clear green pools. The ice is an unreal country of strange images that change continuously as they turn in the currents: arches and bridges, tumbled slabs, bearded old dripping fringes, brown streaks of diatoms trapped in the strata.

At times the ice will bring the cold corpse of a walrus,

145

fatally wounded by native hunters in the north but not recovered, or the gaunt body of a sledge dog. History relates that a half-dozen polar bears have walked in winter to the Pribilofs.

The bull seal is in splendid condition after wintering among the Aleutian Islands, where he moved often from one bay to another to enjoy the shelter of land masses and reefs. He weighs 600 pounds, the limit of size for his kind. His jacket is dark steely gray frosted with white, and his whiskers have been all-white since he turned seven years old. They stem from his upper lip in graceful curves, tapering at the tips and suggesting venerable wisdom in the brain behind them, an effect unsupported by scientific fact. Around his chest and throat are rolls of fat and muscle. He bulges like a wrestler. These masses of flesh are in a sense male sexual organs, for soon he will be called upon to use them as a shield when he fights for breeding territory, and as nourishment during the breeding fast.

He stands on the beach for long minutes, searching the slope of Tolstoi with eyes and nose, studying its geography. All is quiet save for the moaning of the wind and the lapping of the waves among the rotten ice. No sound from another seal, no native voice, serves to guide him home.

As last he moves like a ponderous caterpillar through clean-washed boulders, across snowbanks and gravel beds. He comes to a clearing on the beach that meets his specifications for a breeding ground. He comes to rest on 6 inches of snow and begins to melt his way down to the sand, making an oval nest in the shape of his body.

Watching him with bright, critical eyes from a perch on a crumbling bone is a little brown wren. She often comes to this elevated spot on a moldering pile of skeletons that remain as a memorial to World War One. When the government was looking desperately then for fertilizers, someone suggested that fur-seal bones might be used, and several hundred tons were shipped from the Pribilofs. When news of the Armistice came, the last load was dumped on the ground, and here in the course of time the bones took on the peculiar texture of religious relics, and finally the texture of the tundra soil in which they are now dissolving.

MAY

In early May, reluctant spring moves north and touches the Fur Seal Islands. The organic smells and sounds of Tolstoi increase in volume daily, while the last bergy bits of drift-ice melt into English Bay. The ice front will now retreat to St. Lawrence Island, where the natives will work around the clock hunting the walruses that ride majestically with their newborn calves on the floes. Under the Tolstoi cliff the wrens are singing in full throat, and the longspurs, relatives of the English skylark, are piercing the air with melody as they flutter to the earth. The gulls are circling in confusion, pairing off, quarreling for space, plucking now and then a blade of grass or a frond of seaweed but not yet beginning to nest.

By the first of May, seven bulls have hauled out on Tolstoi, where their scattered shapes are lost among the boulders. By the end of the month their ranks will swell to a hundred, and by the end of June to five hundred. No cows will join them until June. The mood of the bulls is one of tolerance, a cold-war atmosphere of watchful waiting, an uneasy lull before the storm.

In the spring migration, the Golden Seal cuts across the Gulf of Alaska, bypassing Crawfish Inlet in her haste to reach the Pribilofs. She pauses, though, for a full week over Portlock Bank, east of Kodiak, unable to tear herself

away from the food abundance there. What inner pro-
gramming bids her stop and bids her go may never be
known; it is as mysterious as the pacemaker of the biological clock that regulates her feeding hours.

Portlock Bank is 50 miles across. The waters above it
are less than 50 fathoms deep, so the Golden Seal can
easily reach its floor to pursue tasty halibut, cod, flounder,
sole, and other sea-bottom fish. Often, though, she cruises
back and forth in the upper waters where vast numbers
of capelin, sandlance, and pollock drift in shoals. After she
fills her belly she loafs at the surface, in the society of
other seals, sea birds, and porpoises that converge over
the Bank, also with food in mind. When a school of fish
breaks the surface, the gulls, kittiwakes, and murres
materialize above it, and the sight and sound of their
splashing attracts the sea mammals. Though the gulls and
kittiwakes cannot dive, they can strike quickly with their
beaks, impaling a fish 6 inches below the surface. The
murres can dive deeply; the Golden Seal often chases
their silvery outlines as they "fly" awkwardly through the
green water. She has caught and crushed a few of them
in sport but has never tried to swallow them.

It is curious that, among all the pinnipeds, only the
leopard seal of Antarctica depends upon the flesh of
warm-blooded animals for food. The other seals have long
since lost their ancestral taste for land meat—for red
meat. To be sure, an occasional rogue walrus will kill and
eat seals, and a South African fur seal was seen eating

penguins, and the torn body of a ringed seal pup was found in the stomach of a Steller sea lion. These are exceptions to the rule.

On the eighth of May the Golden Seal is rudely interrupted in her feasting by the appearance of an old enemy. She first hears at daybreak the liquid echoes of a ship's propeller, and later sees the silhouette of a schooner, low-down in the loom of Kodiak, then another like it, and another. The halibut season is under way. The crews of the American and Canadian fishing fleets, poised at the ready mark at midnight the night before, are racing to be first on the choicer grounds of Portlock Bank to lay out their miles of setlines, or "skates" of gear. The Golden Seal moves on again along her migratory path.

IN May a biologist arrives at St. Paul Island to prepare for the coming season of research. He has brought from Seattle an invention which he will test as an aid in counting seals and in studying their social use of space. It is a cheap camera suspended from a captive weather-balloon and tripped from the ground by an electric switch. He carries the device to the Reef, inflates the 8-foot balloon with helium, lets it rise to 1200 feet, and snaps the shutter. The camera twists and sways 50 feet below the balloon, jerked by contrary winds. After a dozen snaps, he develops the film, but to his disgust the images are fuzzy. He tries again on a calmer day, but still the motion of the camera defeats his purpose. He decides to shelve the project for another year and meanwhile to think about improvements in design.

On the fifteenth of May, the natives of St. Paul village see a trim white ship come around the Reef and drop her hook in the lee of Tolstoi. She is the *Primus,* of 500 tons, and she is four hours overdue. A motor launch brings her captain to the village dock. "We had a hell of a night," he says, greeting the manager. "We lost a lifeboat and a big chunk out of the laboratory wall."

The *Primus* is a floating workshop for experimental biology and is owned by California Institute. She is staffed by eight physiologists who are busy at the moment repairing the damage of a Bering Sea gale. When a heavy centrifuge tore loose around midnight it charged across the laboratory like a mad bull, turning to kindling whatever it struck. It was brought to a stop by big "Swede" Nelson, who, crouching in pajamas and wretchedly sick, finally roped it to a stanchion.

On the present mission, the scientists of the *Primus* are studying the reactions of arctic animals to cold. They want to know what changes in body form and function have evolved in response to a stressful environment. In pens and cages on the afterdeck are animals already captured: a harbor seal, a sea otter, puffins, petrels and murres from Bogoslof, and king crabs from Kodiak. Now the men hope to find a few Alaska fur seals hauled out in places where they can be approached.

After a night's rest, they drive to Lukanin rookery over roads softened by melting snows. At first glance there are ten or a dozen great bulls lying near the water's edge. One man approaches cautiously and fires a dart syringe from a rifle, but the missile glances off the tough fur coat. A second charge misfires, and by now all the bulls are headed for the sea. This early in the breeding season, before the cows have arrived, the bulls are not aggressive; their innate shyness dominates their territorial imperative. So the men move on to the Reef, where they plan to try a new technique.

The cold metallic sea is breaking heavily on the cold black rocks in the wake of the gale. Swathed in heavy clothes till they resemble huge sausages, five of the men surround a bull and cut him off from the water by tapping his nose lightly with a 10-foot bamboo pole. The peculiar quick flicking of the wooden tip puzzles and frightens him; he moves to a recess in the rocks. Another man now calmly walks to his rump and jabs a syringe into the muscles. There's nothing to it!

For twelve minutes the scene is a *tableau vivant.* Six men stand motionless among the boulders, with the straw-yellow grass behind them. The gray beast all damp with mist is motionless too. Then he begins to make "tasting" movements with his tongue, and to sneeze, and to sway. His voice grows softer. When his 500-pound body dissolves in a lump on the rocks, the men roll him onto a canvas stretcher, truss him like a Christmas goose, and carry him up from the beach. They stagger, and, though the wind is near freezing, they drip with sweat before they get him to the truck.

In the St. Paul laboratory, they stretch him on the floor, wide-eyed but senseless, and begin to measure his blood volume. All the while a trained anesthesiologist kneels beside his snout and administers oxygen when his breathing falters. They inject a measured radioactive tracer into his blood and allow it to circulate for two hours, then withdraw a sample. They estimate, in a scintillation counter, the dilution of the tracer. The end result is 27 quarts of blood, or 10 percent of his body weight. Though the volume could also be measured by draining his blood into a bucket, an unknown percentage would remain in the smaller veins and arteries.

As the bull shows signs of recovering life, the men transport him to a dock, then to a motor-launch, and by superhuman effort to the deck of the *Primus.* Here on the following day they hold him in a metal coffin—a respirometer—and study his breathing chemistry and behavior. He becomes too dangerous to handle, so they finally ease him over the side. He drops with a great splash into the bay and swims drunkenly away, headed for the nearest land.

The scientists return to the Reef and hunt for another

subject. This one proves to be stubborn; he holds out for twenty minutes against the sleep-inducing drug, then drops with a sigh. Before his body temperature can change, a man straddles his back and inserts needle thermometers under the skin of the furred and the naked surfaces.

A driving rain sweeps in from the sea, but the men carry on, huddled around the snoring beast. They suck blue fingers and write on wet notepaper until at last their drooping spirits and their chilling veins compel them to turn stiffly toward the village. The bull regains his power of motion during the night and remembers only that a group of foul-smelling animals entered his territory.

ON the bare face of Tolstoi the lichens and mosses brighten in the growing light of May. During the day, their tiny tissues creep in micro-measurements across the warm rocks, and at night, when the oceanic damp settles down, they rest and drink the dew. They start the parade of northern spring and are followed in succession by more complicated forms of plant and animal life that need more time to unfold and to repair the ravages of winter.

Near the water's edge the air is alive with musical, metallic "clinks." The red phalaropes are back from the far coast of Chile, northward bound for St. Lawrence

Island to nest on the arctic tundra. They are fifty or more, though they twist and turn so quickly on the pebbles and on the shining rain-pools that they seem to be hundreds. They flash in bright rust-red, and black-white-and-gray. They pirouette, dash into pools, and whirl away like corks in a windstorm. Already they are pairing off. Theirs is a strange courtship; the female is larger, more brilliantly colored, and more aggressive than the male. In June, the male will build the nest, a flimsy affair in a clump of grass. The female will lay four eggs therein, and the male will take up the task of incubating and raising the young.

Unconcerned with the origins of their strange way of life, the red phalaropes dance for a while at the edge of Tolstoi and sip the sweet waters of the rain pools. One of them drops lightly to the back of a sleeping seal; another wanders to a clump of grass. *Whiish!*—a gray streak and a spurt of sand, and a white feather slowly falling. The birds lift in alarm and wheel away over the breaking surf. Their excited voices come ever more faintly to the ears of a little fox crunching the trembling body that will not sing again on the nesting plains of the northland.

✦✦✦

IN spring, or in any other season, barren St. Paul Island has little to offer in the way of outdoor recreation to its inhabitants. They tire eventually of the seals and the birds. To be sure, they can always beachcomb, or hunt on the pumice fields for "black diamonds" (attractive little clusters of crystal augite), or gather seal bones to be fashioned into ornaments. On a quiet Saturday, two of the biologists pack their lunches and drive to Cross Hill to mine for walrus ivory. Before the Russians came, thousands of walruses hauled out each year on the Pribilofs. Because they were soon exterminated on the main islands, little is known about them except that nearly all were males. Below Cross Hill, where they habitually rested, and where many of them died of natural causes, the drifting sands gradually entombed them, layer upon layer, in a wilderness catacomb. Whether they died one by one or in a series of catastrophes is a point of argument. According to one theory, several hundred bulls at a time were driven ashore by killer whales. As they struggled in panic to climb the beach, they piled upon one another and suffocated in a hot mass of flesh. Be that as it may, their bones remained under Cross Hill until World War Two, when soldiers stationed here excavated the main walrus mine with a bulldozer and carried off the principal trophies: the tusks and the penis bones. A large specimen of the latter will measure over 20 inches in length and is sure to be a conversation piece when displayed on a hardwood panel in the home of the finder.

The biologists are out for fun today and are also out to tune their muscles for the coming summer's work. With the aid of an old map unknown to the soldiers, they begin to dig at the edge of a grassy hillock marked as a summer camp of the Russian sealers. They carry the sand from the deepening pit by wheelbarrow and shore up the crumbling walls with driftwood. At the end of the day they are 8 feet down and have not found a walrus, though they have struck an ivory comb handcrafted from a tusk, and a sea-otter figurine that might have been a child's plaything a century ago.

They rest their aching backs for a while, leaning against the walls of the old salt house, a weatherbeaten structure that sheltered the native watchmen in the days of Jack London and the fur-seal poachers. The doors and windows have gone with the winds of winter. The rosy finches quarrel now for nesting space along the rafters, and in the quiet gloom the tiny Pribilof shrews run lightly over the brown mold of the floor, lured by the haunting odor of a hundred thousand pelts that long ago dripped their yellow fat into the salt vats.

On Sunday morning the biologists look at blistered hands and make a deal with a native boy to continue the dig. Scarcely has he turned the first shovelful of damp gray sand when he strikes the solid bone of a walrus shoulder-blade. By noon he has uncovered the head with a magnificent pair of tusks of nearly record size, over 32 inches of ivory exposed on the skull. The beast would have been of tremendous size—a size rarely seen today, for the introduction of guns, the outboard motor, and the airplane have brought increased hunting pressure against the walrus herds. It is now the rare bull indeed that lives to become a giant of its kind.

The biologists split the skull neatly down the middle, each taking half. They talk of returning to Cross Hill to dig deeper in the old campsite for artifacts, but on second thought they agree that such a raid would destroy the future value of the place for archaeologists.

JUNE

The dawn comes up fast on the first of June and illuminates the gray form of the great bull, a champion among seals, who planted himself on the beach of Tolstoi in April. He had spent the winter in Bering Sea while weaker members of his class went down to the North Pacific. In April he moved easily back to the rookery, where he took a ringside place at the water's edge. Here he will soon breed more cows than will the late-arriving bulls on the upper slopes, since the females tend to cluster near the sea. His future pups will carry the champion strain, as will their pups, and thus does *Callorhinus* breed from the top of the genetic pool. The pace of evolution is most rapid in the bloodlines of the noblest individuals.

Along the sea for a thousand yards, the front-line places are now filled with bulls. The ones that come later will have to fight their way through the line or else sneak around to upper levels. A soft breeze carries the grassy fragrance of the stirring tundra across the face of the rookery to mingle with the morning mists from the beach. The wild birds above fly north. The bulls are restless; they pace their small kingdoms and growl softly to themselves. An unseen current holds them together in bonds of mutual distrust.

A hundred feet from the gray seal, a black bull of nearly equal size drifts quietly toward the shore of English Bay. His flippers are limp; his body turns lightly with the waves. With nose pointing cautiously toward the land, he comes to rest on a submerged rock in the tidal zone— only another black body among the black rounded rocks. A swish of the surf and he is an animated lump on the beach. He gives a gargling cry of success—the first exercise of voice since December.

Gray Bull is up in a flash, trying to identify the source of the call and its echo somewhere near his station. He is the "champion ringed about with enemies." He sees Black Bull. He charges with a rolling gait like a broad-shouldered circus horse. The action freezes as the pair approach within a yard of each other's teeth; they stare obliquely, as though embarrassed at the confrontation. Black Bull utters a harsh rasping pant; Gray Bull answers with a rattling growl. Other bulls take up the chorus, as they will again and again a hundred times before the breeding season is over. They growl in sympathy, triggered by feelings over which they have no control. Black Bull sidles around to place his thin-skinned and defenseless rump uphill, but Gray Bull counters, and once more they stand shoulder to shoulder, facing in opposite directions.

All at once the pent-up emotions generated by the feel of solid ground underfoot and the hot musky breath of a rival push the newcomer into action. Like a striking snake his bared teeth flash toward the tender armpit of the other, but as he flattens his body, Gray Bull drops his own shoulder and the water flies in a wet cloud from

162

Black Bull's neck. They push furiously against each other, each trying to upset the other's balance. They separate and stand apart for a minute, alternately roaring and giving off shrill, piping whistles, while their fat bodies seem to swell with rage. Another and more serious attack leaves Black Bull holding a loose fold of Gray Bull's neck firmly in his jaws. The tension mounts as the bulls grow hot and silent except for gasping breath.

Once more the scene is a blur of flipper upon flipper, sand spurting in all directions, white teeth recurved and flashing in the air, loose fur drifting down the breeze. They disengage. Blood pours from a deep gutter on Gray Bull's neck and dribbles down his chest, clotting darkly.

The match is an even one. It rages for twenty minutes, while new blood shows in streaks on the flippers of the antagonists and the angry foam of saliva flecks their jackets. Toward the end, their actions become mechanical. The bulls pretend to strike, then draw back at the last moment. When they lock in combat they freeze like weary wrestlers waiting for breath to return. At last the decision goes to Gray Bull on staying power—power of will as well as muscle. In the role of defender against aggressor, he has held a psychological advantage. Black Bull rushes headlong up the slope, giving a high-pitched whine as he disappears. He passes safely between the territories of bulls in the second rank and finds a quiet place to cool his heated body. There he sits patient of injury. He does not lick his wounds as a dog would, but lets the blood clot, the dirt enter the cuts, and the bluebottle flies lay eggs in the festering sores . . . and he lives to fight again.

On the deserted battlefield a little fox with hungry eyes, a vixen with belly drooping from unborn young, creeps from the shelter of a boulder and nibbles at the bloody sand.

Off to the south, where the rookery rises in terraces to a high cliff and where the late-arriving seals are working their way inland around the ends of the first-line defenders, the contagion of battle has spread to a pair of young bulls. Thus far, the contest is all display. A nine-year-old (of placid disposition) and an eight-year-old (more truculent) are engaged in a show of bluff. They prance about and skirmish without body contact. Each goes through his repertoire of nasty threats, ending in a loud explosion like the sound of an old-fashioned engine driving a wood-saw: "puh—puh—ha-ha-ha!" Neither bull has settled on a territory for the coming season; each is defending an idea rather than a home. Each is well acquainted with the rules of the game, having practiced the appropriate sounds and movements from his first summer of life.

Without warning, a third bull now enters the arena, a dirty brown fellow bearing the scars of many contests. His left eye is marble white, blinded by an old infection, and the side of his face is scarred by a permanent sneer. Half-blind though he is, he does not hesitate. In two galloping bounds he looms above the placid bull and begins to whip him with his teeth. The younger bull sinks in surprise, then rolls among the boulders like a worm on a hot pavement. When he gains the safety of a gap, the big bull turns on the other one and drives him without mercy to the edge of a cliff. Over he goes! Twenty feet below on solid basalt he lands with a dull thud and lies like dead, then rises stiffly and slides into the cool sea.

✦ ✦ ✦

IN June the summer people start to swarm on the Pribilof Islands along with the seals, though for different reasons. Some are here to study the animals, some to help with the seal-killing, and others to build the roads and houses that seem never to keep up with the growing native population.

One of the new arrivals is a parasitologist who has spent several years in a futile effort to unlock the mystery of the fur-seal hookworm. Where does it spend the winter, only to resume its deadly cycle in June when the first pups are born? The hookworm is a thready white worm that multiplies in the intestine, drills through the wall, and brings death by internal bleeding. It may strike quickly, leaving a fat pup dead on the beach with its belly still full of milk. Early in his study the parasitologist had found the living larvae in the frozen winter soil of the rookeries where, according to all the textbooks, hookworms cannot survive. So he drenched experimental plots of ground with carbolic acid and other poisons before the seals arrived in summer, and still the pups died by the tens of thousands. With his sharp scissors, the scientist went through miles of guts but never found a worm in seals older than pups.

Now in desperation he decides to put aside all previous notions about the life history of hookworms in dogs and humans and other animals, and to think afresh. The *Anna B* is sealing near the Pribilofs, so he asks by radio for a carcass of an adult female seal. It arrives the next day and he starts to go through the blubber layer. Here is a rich find: quiescent hookworm larvae by the hundreds in the fat of the mammary gland. A few weeks later, when the first pups are dropped, he looks in their stomach contents and finds that, with the first milk she gives her baby, the mother unwittingly infects it with the worm. Whether it lives or dies will be resolved by its ability to develop immunity. If it survives, and most pups do, it will never again harbor the worm in its gut, though it will carry the sleeping larvae in its blubber for life.

✦✦✦

TWO months have now gone by since the first bull crawled uncertainly onto the snows of Tolstoi on the thirteenth of April. Now the rookery is nearly filled with bulls

166

on station, row upon row in a regular pattern aligned with the seashore. Those animals that are lying prone, with flippers tucked under belly, are facing inland, because at this season the chance of an attack by rivals is more likely to come from the plateau, where most of the seals destined to remain "idle" or "unemployed" are waiting to do battle. The bulls not lying prone are sitting on their heels, turning their heads in suspicion at each new sound.

During the next four months the rookery will not be silent for a moment. Three old cows, all of them pregnant, hauled out on the beach before daybreak on the thirteenth of June. The first females to return, they all gathered near a bull who was guarding a station on a rotting mass of kelp within the wash of the tides. He was electrified. Now he circles the cows without rest, "whickering" at intervals, and watching for competitors, for he is in a vulnerable spot. The cows ignore him except to snarl or to touch him whisker-to-whisker when he brushes against them. Each one sleeps with her head thrown back, neck folded in a curve, eyes closed, stirring from time to time when she feels the impatient life in her womb. In the afternoon, and during the night, and in the days to come, other females will arrive by the scores and hundreds, then a thousand a day until more than twenty thousand breeding cows are coming and going across the sands of Tolstoi.

The Golden Seal moves with steady purpose through the Sandman Reefs, her eyes fixed on the west. Her body bulges awkwardly and she finds swimming a little harder each day. She is 400 miles from home, but if all goes well she will make it in June, a week earlier than in the year before.

She cannot know that killers are waiting in Unimak Pass.

Around four in the afternoon she pauses like a dust mote in a vast empty chamber. Forty feet below the top of the sea her body is weightless and formless, a dark interruption in a universe of blue. Though her eyes are open she does not see. Small captive bubbles fall upward from furry pockets in her coat. She is near that state which consists of doing nothing at all. Often in the afternoons, floating at the level of least effort, she will rest in this fashion for three or four minutes at a time.

Now a subtle change in illumination breaks her trance and she becomes again a seal with a mission. She rises underneath a school of gray-and-yellow fish and bites the first one with an easy snap. Too late she knows the stinging truth! The fish are little prowfish, traveling by habit below the pale umbrella of an orange jellyfish 2 feet in diameter. Hanging from it are long, translucent tentacles, slender, ghostly, pulsing softly and bearing thousands of poisonous darts.

The Golden Seal doubles in pain as though struck by a flame. She speeds through the cool water. Within moments, her eyes are swollen shut, and not until evening of the following day is she back to normal.

Her mistake can be laid to haste alone, since she knows by heart the ordinary dangers of the sea. Jellyfishes of great variety—brown, orange, white, and blue—have been a part of her aquatic world since the days of her puppyhood, and she has learned to avoid the poisonous kinds (most of the time), as a farm boy early learns to know the thorns and nettles along his path.

On the sixteenth of June at 3:49 in the morning the red sun rises from a crack at the edge of the sea and begins to paint the ceiling of clouds over Tolstoi rookery. On the beach below, a female seal begins to jerk her body convulsively and to crawl in tight circles as though responding to a message hidden in the light of the distant sky. She turns with an air of bewilderment and nuzzles the base of her tail. She is a lonely female animal about to begin that dark journey from which there is no turning back; she is about to give birth. There will be no witnesses, no records in a book. She is all alone with the sea wind, and the sand, and the pain. She bends her pearl-gray head sharply over her back and looks at a pale blue sack that starts to balloon from her vaginal opening. A gush of liquid wets the sand and a black nose appears, then a black head that grows as she watches. She bites it gently. At the constriction of the neck, the little body stays its progress for a long minute. The mother tramples the ground, twists her rump, and waves her flippers wildly in the air. All in a moment, it lies there in the morning light—a black thing that bleats, and swims on the sand with slate-gray flippers, and blinks its eyes, and shakes a head too large for its body, and shivers as though it would never stop. The umbilical cord still links it with the mother's body. She makes no effort to align herself with her rear toward the pup to ease the passage of the afterbirth. She lies for a while on her belly and wrists, dozing, with eyes closed. She is desperately tired. Then she rouses and walks a few paces up the beach, dragging the pup behind her. When the placenta frees itself she turns quickly, as though all at once she had caught the meaning of the play, and begins to press her nose in rising excitement against the steaming form of her baby.

Even as she does so, another baby on another beach sees the light . . . and then another. The procession which will bring the summer recruits to the Pribilof herd by the end of August is under way.

THE tempo of human life also quickens on St. Paul Island in June. The sealing gang comes out from the village for a workout on the beach of English Bay. Their tools are clean and bright. One of the men is new on the job, promoted from the ranks of sticker. Ka-wa—Sea Lion —they call him, because of his barrel chest and thighs like tree trunks. He grips his club in his sweaty hands, determined to show his skill at this child's play, but he overcompensates. As he prods a big six-year-old, the beast seizes the club in angry teeth and jerks it from his hands, swings it in a quick circle and strikes poor Ka-wa on the side of the head. The pain is minor compared to the ridicule he will suffer as the first man to have been clubbed by a seal.

Women and old men and sleepy-eyed children from the village have risen before dawn to watch the first kill of the season and are standing on a hillside out of danger's way. As the kill progresses and the rows of naked carcasses begin to show obscenely in the wake of the gang, a few old men come down to the trampled grass and begin to salvage edible parts, especially livers, hearts, and tongues. A boy moves along the rows in a crouching motion, engaged in a most peculiar business that will yield him several hundred dollars before the summer is over; he is cutting "seal sticks." With one hand he grasps the genital organs of the male seals, severs them from the body with a knife, and plops them into a sack. Later, he will clean and trim them, hang them on netting to dry, and eventually ship them to San Francisco for sale to the "oriental medicine" market. Whether or not the organs contain a restorative element depends upon the faith of the user.

Another boy clambers over the wet, bloody hummocks of grass, holding a butcher knife as long as his forearm. He is cutting the stoutest whiskers from the carcasses, to be sold in San Francisco for a penny apiece. Dark rumor has it that the whiskers are exactly right in stiffness and flexibility for the cleaning of opium pipes.

After the kill is over, two biologists and a native begin

the annual count of bull seals, a routine job which, in the next five days, will take them to vantage points where they can look down upon 95 percent of the adult male seals of the Pribilof Islands. Of all the counts and estimates of seal population, this one is the most reliable. The dark shapes of the bulls loom above the lesser forms of the females, and the bulls stay in one place, which further helps in counting them. For sixty years, the "bull census" has been a valuable index of the rise and fall of the seal population. During the count, the biologists keep separate tallies of idle bulls and harem bulls and draw inferences from the yearly change in the relationship between them. As long as the harem bulls outnumber the idles two to one, the herd is thought to be in healthy balance.

When the men approach the catwalk above Tolstoi, they find their way blocked by an enormous, quick-tempered bull who has planted himself at the entrance. They whip him lightly about the face with their bamboo poles, but he will not be moved. Toadlike, here he has waited for a month and here he will stay. In red-eyed anger he jerks a pole in his teeth and tears it to splinters. The men pelt him with rocks. They try to climb the catwalk by another route, but he looms above them in a rush. Finally the leader takes a pistol from his pack and turns inquiringly to a companion, who replies to the unspoken word: "Why not? We can use him for a specimen." A pistol is carried routinely to arouse sleeping bulls for the head-count. When it is fired above the rookery, the air is quiet for a moment, then the dawn chorus of a thousand

172

gargling throats resounds in greater volume. So a shot rings out, and twenty minutes later the men continue with the counting.

Later in the day they use the empty stomach of the bull to estimate its food capacity. They tie a string around the outlet, fill the stomach with tap water, and measure the volume. It amounts to 10 quarts, or 39 pounds. Knowing that body tissues are always relaxed in death, they estimate that the stomach of a living seal would perhaps hold half this amount, or 20 pounds.

During the annual June inventory of breeding stock, they have a chance, as at no other time of the year, to see intimately some of the little dramas of seal behavior that are continuously being played on a thousand stages. They see a mother with the head of a pup protruding from her swollen body, both animals dead. They watch a copulation in which the female is oddly submissive. After the bull descends, they visit the scene and find that his mate has been dead for a week. They watch with amusement as a little pup struggles for five minutes to crawl over a gray porous boulder that it could easily walk around, and they wonder at its perseverance. They conclude that stubbornness in seals may have no value to the race and may, in fact, be one of those blind alleys that lead off at every turn in the path of evolution. As they sit, philosophizing, upon the planking of the catwalk, they hear a sudden commotion and see one bull fleeing from the territory of another. He rushes over the broken ground until he reaches the struggling pup, when he pauses, and in a spirit of what might be frustrated aggressiveness, seizes the little thing, shakes it with frightful violence, and hurls it through the air. It spins wildly for a distance of 50 feet, then drops and lies without moving; it dies rapidly and quietly.

In mid-afternoon the sea breeze falls away and leaves the rookery quiet, warm and suffused with gray light pouring down from a hazy overcast. The men are suddenly conscious of the rank smell of guano in their surroundings. They watch a black pup wade aimlessly into a stinking pool of rainwater and emerge, dripping with brown slime, on the opposite bank. They muse over the fact that seals have lost all the sanitary instincts that are still possessed by dogs and cats and other land-animal relatives. Seals are roving animals and, like horses and cows, are not toilet-trained. By contrast, the little field-mouse that day after day must tread on the same runways through the grass has developed the habit of leaving its body wastes in neat piles at regular stations along the way. The biologists conclude that seals are oblivious of body wastes, neither avoiding them nor using them, as some animals do, as recognition marks or scent stations.

Visitors to the Pribilof Islands in summer are often surprised to find the seals so healthy and active in view of the filthy environment in which they live and in view of their total unconcern for cleanliness. Many zoologists, too, have wondered about the vigor of the seals but have not been able to explain it. Perhaps some day the seals will suffer an epizootic when a visitor brings a new pathogen to the islands, or when a seal in migration toward land picks up a stray organism from a germ-warfare test in the North Pacific.

Late in June, three biologists succeed in a task they have fumbled in earlier trials—milking a seal and getting enough pure milk for chemical study. With the stage all set in the laboratory, they go to the Reef and wait quietly at the end of the rookery until they see a female come in from the sea dripping wet, her belly sagging with milk destined for a pup somewhere on the beach. When she has cleared the front line of harems and is crossing an open space, they rush her with lariats in hand and pin her to the ground. They inject a tranquilizing drug, lash her quickly to a stretcher, and within ten minutes have her in the laboratory. Here they strap her to a wooden table provided with openings adjustable to the pattern of her teats. One man lies on his back under the table, struggles to place a beaker under each of her breasts, and struggles further to pull each black little nipple from its depression in the skin. Another man injects a relaxing drug designed to start the letting down of milk, drop by drop. When the milk flow slackens off at a total yield of one-third pint, the men are satisfied. They return the frightened mother to the rookery to rendezvous with her pup and to continue the release of milk at her own pace.

THE shining peak of Shishaldin, 9,000 feet above the sea, fades in the distant sky as the weary Golden Seal turns the corner into Unimak Pass and heads for Bering Sea. She is fully alert in the treacherous confines of the Pass, for here the maelstroms pull and the sudden tides rake the ragged rocks. Forbidding cliffs loom and disappear in the swirling mists, while slimy tendrils of seaweed ebb and flow in a frenzy of motion and the voices of the wild creatures moving through the Pass sound and resound from hidden reefs and ledges. The Golden Seal keeps pace with four other pregnant females and a young-adult male who, though sexually mature, will not be able to win a place on the breeding ground this year. His bright new mane is a clear indication that he has recently come of age.

As the six animals with a common destination thread their way through the reefs near Kaligagan Island they begin to hear faintly the sound that chills the blood of all seals in all oceans: the distant talk of a pack of killer whales. The source is unclear; it is several miles away, and the message is deflected in its underwater travel by the rugged contours of the Pass. The seals have no choice but to press on. Within a half-hour they know that the pack is behind them and is closing rapidly. No whale or seal is swifter than the killer.

176

JUNE

Back in the rising fog the dorsal fins of the killers leave V-shaped wakes on the sea, the tracks of seven females, a calf, and a bull. The yellowish markings on the back of the calf and the shallow creases along its flanks show that it is only a few weeks old. A mile away from the pack, a lone bull killer is attracting attention for some reason or another, hurling himself time and again into the air until only his tail flukes are dragging, then falling on his side with a tremendous *whoosh!* and a fountain of spray. The pack now feeding in the Pass has been loitering here for several weeks, drawn by the Steller sea lions that are giving birth on the Aleutian rocks, and by the tens of thousands of fur seals migrating through the Pass. The whales snort loudly, give off squeals that carry down the wind for a thousand yards, and enjoy a continuous underwater discussion so complex phonetically that it surely must be a language, though not yet decoded by man.

Not until the killers are within sight of the Golden Seal do they turn in her direction. The bull slides beneath the surface like a torpedo, reappearing after five long minutes, incredibly, with a young male seal held crosswise in his jaws! He plunges in and out of the sea for twenty minutes, tossing the paralyzed animal high into the air as a cat would play with a mouse, until he finally severs its spine and releases it from pain and terror.

The Golden Seal is wild with fright. She propels her pregnant body to the absolute limit of its power, blindly and without reason, heading back in the direction from whence she came, until the sounds of the killers fade away. Another female dodges the repeated slashes of a killer's jaws, but loses both hind flippers in the process. She escapes to a quiet channel in the kelp where she gives birth prematurely to a pup that sees the new world for a few minutes before it drowns, and she, too, hovers at the door of death for a week before she strokes on to the Pribilofs, trailing the white stumps of her ankles.

Six fur seals at ten o'clock—two seals and four stains in the water of the Pass at ten-thirty. The calendar turns inflexibly toward the end of the year of the seal.

On the final day, a rainstorm whips the face of Tolstoi. Brown rivulets flow across the shining rocks and sink into the sand and drip into the sea. As the storm fades, the Golden Seal comes riding home on the torn discolored waters. She creeps through a curtain of iridescent foam and stops in sudden pain in the tidal zone beside a yellow log that, like herself, has come to rest on land. Minutes pass; then comes the cry of her newborn pup. . . .

APPENDIX: On the Origin of Seals

What point in time was the point of no return for seals? When did their ancestors depart from the line of proto-bears and dawn-otters and other flesh-eating beasts of the Tertiary continents? What limy skulls have been brought to light from ancient rocky beds?

A few geologists, but only a few, have been caught up in the excitement of tracing the genealogy of seals. To reconstruct an ancient seal, they must find a fossil outcrop in a marine sediment, chisel it roughly from the mother rock, and spend weeks in the laboratory laying bare the bones and teeth, millimeter by millimeter, with a sandblasting tool as delicate as an artist's brush.

The Alaska fur seal is one of thirty-three species of pinnipeds, or seals in the broad sense, and these are members of a larger fraternity, the marine mammals. The ancestors of all marine mammals long ago lived on land. Overwhelming evidence from the fossil record shows that the earliest vertebrates, or animals with backbones, were fishes. Some of them gave rise to the amphibians (including modern frogs and salamanders), and some of the amphibians later gave rise to the reptiles (including modern snakes, lizards, turtles, and alligators). About 180 million years ago, near the end of the Triassic period, some of the reptiles gave rise to the first mammals. These were no larger than rats and mice.

In the long millennia down to the present time, the mammals "experimented" with hundreds of thousands of different shapes and habits. Some species moved underground and others into the air, into trees and onto grasslands, into swamps and freshwater lakes, and into the sea. Meanwhile, a few reptiles not ancestral to the mammalian line grew adept at living in the sea. The ichthyosaurs and plesiosaurs attained a length of 30 feet; they swam with paddle-shaped limbs; they resembled modern whales and might have become whales, but they did not. They disappeared in the Cretaceous period—the time of the great dying—when so many other reptiles vanished.

No fossils have ever been found which, by any stretch of the imagination, could have linked the successful marine reptiles of the Cretaceous with the successful marine mammals of the present. On the contrary, the record shows that, after the land mammals finally came into their own, some species became dabblers in the sea; they persisted in tapping its food riches farther and farther from shore. To be sure, some of them failed. The bones of a sea-going raccoon-bear (*Kolponomos*) were found in a cliff above Juan de Fuca Strait. But some were successful, and these are the true marine mammals of

182

today: the sea otter, the pinnipeds, the sirenians (manatees and dugongs), and the cetaceans (whales and dolphins).

The four groups represent four distances in time from land ancestors, and the hands and feet of their members are a living clue to the distance. The sea otter as a marine mammal is only 2 million years old; its front paws are rather ordinary, its hind feet are flippers. The pinnipeds are at least 30 million years old; all four of their limbs end in flippers. The sirenians are at least 80 million years old; their hind limbs have disappeared entirely; their arms end in flippers which can be manipulated for holding food and the nursling calf. The cetaceans are at least 100 million years old; their hind limbs also have disappeared; their flippered arms are rigid from the shoulder outward.

Why use the term "true" marine mammals? By definition, these have two exclusive features: they depend entirely on living food gathered beneath the surface of the sea, and none can mate with any land mammal. These features separate them from mammals like the polar bear, the Cape Horn otters, and the fish-eating bats of Trinidad and Mexico, which only dabble in the sea and along its shores. The polar bear in captivity will readily mate with the brown bear.

Besides their exclusive features, the true marine mammals have features which they share with other animals. Thus, they make no den or nest and they give birth in the open to a single, well-developed offspring; so does the antelope. They all have flippers; so does the sea turtle.

183

With the exception of the sea otter, they all have blubber; so does the hippopotamus.

Exceptions to the rule can be ignored. Some "marine" mammals live the year around in freshwater lakes or streams. These, however, are offshoots of predominantly marine groups, and they closely resemble their salt-water relatives. Lake Baikal, in Siberia, has a resident population of eighty thousand small, unspotted, gray-coated seals that resemble the ringed seals of the Arctic Ocean but have never tasted salt water. According to one theory, the lake seals are still living in the ancestral homeland of relatives who long ago went to sea. The Baikal seals originated from an otter-like land animal, developed the features they now display, and kept these conservative features in the unchanging environment of a deep, isolated lake. But some individuals are believed to have escaped to the ocean, where their descendants split into many species, and spread to many ecological niches, and gradually assumed many shapes and habits fitting them to the new niches. However, wherever they went from pole to pole, and however bizarre the shapes they adopted, they retained one conspicuous heritage: they continued to crawl on their bellies. A second group of modern seals includes the fur seals, the sea lions, and the walruses. These are able to walk on all fours. So today the pinnipeds are classified in two groups: the crawlers (Phocoidea), of presumed otterlike origin, and the walkers (Otarioidea) of presumed bearlike origin.

The fossil evidence of seal ancestry does not reveal

whether the family tree had one trunk or two. Some zoologists (and I among them) believe that two stocks of land carnivores went to sea independently at widely separated places and then gave rise to the crawlers and the walkers. Others believe that a single stock of proto-seals made the sea passage and then split into two groups.

New evidence from the study of living chromosomes supports the latter, or one-trunk theory. A bit of skin tissue, say from a walrus, is packed in ice and airmailed to a laboratory where it is transplanted to a miniature "hot bed" of nutrient broth. After a few days, a transparent film of new skin, one cell deep, begins to grow and spread on the glass substrate of the garden. The tissue is then killed, stained, and squashed under pressure, whereupon the chromosomes in each cell move apart and reveal their individual shapes and sizes. Every species of animal in the world has a characteristic chromosome pattern, or karyotype, which identifies it and also shows its relation—close or distant—to other animals. In all of the seal karyotypes studied up to now, the number of chromosomes is thirty-two to thirty-six.

At no time in history or in geologic prehistory have fur seals bred in North Atlantic waters. They originated in the North Pacific and later colonized the southern hemisphere by drifting southward along the eastern shore of the Pacific basin. Strangely, when they had rounded Cape Horn into the South Atlantic and had turned northward, they did not try again to penetrate tropical waters but stopped at southern Brazil.

185

In order to complete, as it were, an unfinished work of nature, several biologists have suggested that fur seals be transplanted to the North Atlantic, to islands off the coast of Newfoundland. They would breed on land, of course, and would winter among the fishing fleets of the Grand Bank. Other biologists are not keen on the proposal, for they have an uneasy feeling that if fur seals were dropped into this long-established, complex natural environment, they would displace some equally useful and interesting creatures.

If the "success" of a living organism is defined as its ability to multiply and spread over the earth, the crawling seals must be given a higher rating than the walking seals. The world population of crawlers is about sixteen million, while that of the walkers is only four million.

To speculate whether one kind of seal is "higher" or "lower" than another in the natural order of life is only a semantic game, for there is no good definition of evolutionary progress. Every seal—and every other mammal except man—has gone about as far as it can toward perfection within its environmental niche. The powerful influence of natural selection is now more effective in stabilizing specific gains than in improving upon them.

World environments will surely change in the future as they have in the past. If the changes are gradual, species will adapt, and if they are abrupt, species will die. While Lake Tanganyika in Southeast Africa, during millions of years, turned from salt water to fresh, some of the native jellyfish, but none of the starfish, changed in shape and body chemistry to fit the new situation.

Conceivably, a hundred generations of men could breed back a stock of captive fur seals into bear-like beasts resembling the hypothetical Eocene ancestor of both seals and bears, but if the job were left to Nature alone, she would never bring it off. Each tiny backward step would bring the fur seal closer to competition in the wild with the real bears now successfully occupying the "bear niche" on land.

The British zoologist Julian Huxley has offered a definition of biological progress or improvement with which many zoologists agree. (In the long run a definition of "improvement" will be agreed upon rather than discovered.) It is, he says, "that particular type . . .which is free from restrictions and limitations, or in other words permits further improvements." It is a definition very close to "freedom."

REFERENCE NOTES

PAGE & LINE

3:*1–11*   Rudyard Kipling, *The Jungle Books* (New York: Macmillan, 1964), p. 252.

4:*18–24*   W. Turton (ed.), *A General System of Nature through the Three Grand Kingdoms . . . by Sir Charles Linne . . .* (London: Lackington, Allen and Co., 1806), vol. 1, p. 38.

6:*13–23*   Leonhard Stejneger, *Georg Wilhelm Steller: The Pioneer of Alaskan Natural History* (Cambridge: Harvard University Press, 1936), pp. 278–281, 358–361. See also pp. 193-194 of the present book.

7:*18*
through
8:*2*   St. George, the southern island of the Pribilof group, was discovered in the summer of 1786; St. Paul, the northern island, in 1786 or 1787. Of several vague or conflicting accounts, perhaps the best is Martin Sauer's *An Account of a Geographical and Astronomical Expedition to the Northern Parts of Russia . . . by Commodore Joseph Billings in the Years 1785, etc., to 1794; the Whole Narrated from the Original Papers* (London: T. Cadell, Jun., and W. Davies, 1802), p. 210. Sauer and Pribilof met at Unalaska in 1790.

PAGE & LINE

16:*10–11*   Homer, *The Odyssey,* Book IV, lines 404–406, as translated in Robert Hamilton, *Amphibious Carnivora* (London: Henry G. Bohn, 1860), p. 263.

21:*2–3*   Robert Falcon Scott, *Scott's Last Expedition* (New York: Dodd, Mead, 1913), p. 415.

34:*14–15*   G. C. L. Bertram, "Pribilof Fur Seals," *Arctic,* vol. 3, no. 2 (1950), p. 77.

51:*9ff.*   California Institute is fictitious. It represents an imaginary private nonprofit research organization supported by private and government funds. The experiments on captive seals described here are drawn mainly from Charles E. Rice (ed.), *The Behavior and Physiology of Pinnipeds* (New York: Appleton-Century-Crofts, 1968), and Harald T. Andersen (ed.), *The Biology of Marine Mammals* (New York: Academic Press, 1969).

63:*19–21*   Charles Bryant was the first special agent of the U. S. Treasury Department on the Pribilof Islands, where he landed in March 1869. His story of fur seal pups eaten by killer whales has never been substantiated; it appears in David Starr Jordan (ed.), *The Fur Seals and the Fur-Seal Islands* . . . , part 2, p. 506. (For complete bibliographic data, see p. 196 of the present book.)

78:*7ff.*   The "observations" at Kitovi are a composite based on studies made by Victor B. Scheffer in 1950 (unpublished), by George A. Bartholomew (department of zoology, University of California at Los Angeles) in 1951, and by Richard S. Peterson (division of natural sciences, University of California at Santa Cruz) in 1961-1963. For further information, see Peterson's *Social Behavior*

REFERENCE NOTES

PAGE & LINE

in Pinnipeds with Particular Reference to the Northern Fur Seal, in Rice, *The Behavior and Physiology of Pinnipeds,* op. cit., pp. 3–53.

87:*10ff.*   Nick, Feodor, Dorofy, and Ivan are fictitious.

87:*15*   The "Seattle Laboratory" is the Marine Mammal Biological Laboratory, Bureau of Commercial Fisheries, Fish and Wildlife Service, U S. Department of the Interior, in Seattle, Washington.

88:*3–22*   Ward T. Bower, "Alaska Fishery and Fur Seal Industries in 1919," U. S. Commissioner of Fisheries *Report for 1919* (Bureau of Fisheries *Document* no. 891), appendix 9, p. 75. Four war-surplus tractors were sent to St. Paul Island in 1919 when A. H. Proctor was agent and caretaker of the island.

108:*21–28*   Randall R. Howard, "Dynamiting Sea Lions," *Technical World Magazine,* vol. 20, no. 3 (1913), pp. 365–366.

108:*28*
through   J. McHugh, "Hair Seals," Canada Department of Naval Service, Fisheries Branch, *Fiftieth Annual Report,*
109:*8*   (1918), pp. 235–237.

116:*13*   Though the North Pacific Fur Seal Commission is real,
through   and it first convened in Washington, D.C., in November
118:*8*   1957, the present story of a "meeting" is a composite designed to suggest the spirit of the annual meetings.

117:*27–29*   North Pacific Fur Seal Commission, . . . *Report on Investigations from 1964 to 1966* (Issued from the headquarters of the Commission, Washington, D.C., 1969), p. 13.

129:*2 ff.*   *Anna B* is fictitious. The objectives and methods of pelagic sealing for research purposes are explained in North

Pacific Fur Seal Commission, *Report on Investigations from 1958 to 1961*, pp. 1–3. (For complete bibliographic data see p. 199 of the present book.)

135:*1*   *Catalyst* is fictitious.

135:*28*   Vita-Fare is fictitious.

152:*9ff.*   All names in the story of the *Primus* are fictitious, but the account is based on the cruise of the *Alpha Helix*, of Scripps Institution of Oceanography, La Jolla, California, in the spring of 1968.

187:*8–10*   Julian Huxley, *The Evolutionary Process*, in Julian Huxley, A. C. Hardy, and E. B. Ford (eds.), *Evolution as a Process* (London: George Allen and Unwin, 1954), p. 13.

SEVEN ACCOUNTS OF THE FUR SEAL:
A Selected and Annotated Bibliography

No book contains the full story of the Alaska fur seal, but it has been written piecemeal in popular articles, technical and scientific reports, and government documents. The following accounts, published between 1751 and 1954, are historically important for their contribution to knowledge of the seal and to the conservation of its species.

GEORG WILHELM STELLER. "De Bestiis Marinis" [Beasts of the Sea], in *Novi Commentarii Academiae Scientarum Imperialis Petropolitanae*, vol. 2 (for the year 1749, published 1751), pp. 289-398 (often catalogued as *Akademiia Nauk, Memoires*, series 2, vol. 2). Partial translation by Walter Miller and Jennie Emerson Miller in part 3 of *The Fur Seals and Fur-Seal Islands of the North Pacific Ocean* (see page 196).

Steller, later recognized as the pioneer of Alaskan natural history, was a member of Vitus Bering's 1741 expedition to search for a land connection between Asia and America. On November 5, the packet boat in which Steller and Bering were traveling was wrecked on Bering Island. Here Bering and Steller spent the following eight months. In the intervals of caring for the sick, burying the dead, carving out shelters in the snow-covered tundra, and hunting for food,

193

Steller made the notes which included the first descriptions of mammals now known as the northern fur seal, Steller sea lion, sea otter, and Steller sea cow to be published in Europe. His first mention of a seal was in connection with the killing of an old bull on April 29, 1742. On May 28 he took thirty-one measurements of a large bull, dissected it, and described it. In addition to the essential details of fur-seal biology, his work also contains two pictures of seals believed to have been made on the spot by a draftsman with the expedition. After the survivors returned to Kamchatka, Steller wrote an introduction to his notes and forwarded the whole manuscript to the Academy of Sciences in St. Petersburg. It was read before the Academy in May 1747. The author had died in Siberia the previous year at the age of thirty-seven.

IOANN VENIAMINOV (INNOKENTII). "Morskoi Kot" [The Sea Bear], in *Wrangell's Nachrichten über die Russischen Besitzungen an der Nordwestküste von Amerika* [Wrangell's Information on the Russian Possessions on the Northwest Coast of America]. St. Petersburg: Buchdruckerei der Kaiserlichen Akademie der Wissenschaften, 1839. Translation by Leonard Stejneger in part 3 of *The Fur Seals and Fur-Seal Islands of the North Pacific Ocean* (see page 196).

Veniaminov was sent as a missionary to Unalaska in the Aleutian Islands in 1825 and at some time paid a visit to the Pribilof Islands. In addition to his churchly duties, he translated the Aleut language into Russian, kept weather records, and described the life of the Aleuts. In 1840 he was appointed bishop of a diocese that included all the Russian Orthodox churches in Russian America, with headquarters at Sitka; at that time he took the name Innokentii. Later he returned to Russia to become metropolitan of Moscow. Although Russian fur seekers had been exploiting the great seal herd on the Pribilofs since 1786, almost nothing was recorded about the seals until Veniaminov's work appeared. He added little to Steller's description of fur-seal

194

biology: his main contribution was to describe for the first time the Russian methods of harvesting seals. Everyone—men, women, and children—took part in the sealing drives, which began in late September, after the molting season rather than before, as is the present practice. Then as now, the main sealing effort was directed at the bachelor males, but "the quite young seals . . . only four months of age [were] killed"—not for their skins, however; the meat of the pups, salted or dried, was the Pribilof natives' chief source of food until well into the nineteenth century. Veniaminov reported that more than three million seal skins were taken from the Pribilofs during the first forty-eight years of Russian exploitation.

HENRY WOOD ELLIOTT. *Report on the Prybilov Group, or Seal Islands, of Alaska.* Washington, D.C.: Government Printing Office, 1874.

Elliott first saw the Pribilof Islands, then under Russian rule, in 1865, as a nineteen-year-old artist-naturalist assigned by the Smithsonian Institution to the Western Union Telegraph Expedition; his last visit to them was in 1913, as a special agent for a congressional committee in search of evidence of government corruption. In 1926 he appeared before another congressional committee to repeat charges of government skullduggery. During the sixty-one years he followed the fortunes of the seals, his name occurred over and over in the annals of sealing. The chief significance of this book lies in the fact that it was the first designed to tell the American people about its recently acquired resource, the fur-seal herd. "Designed" is used advisedly. The author later referred to the work as a "report of mine made upon the Prybilov Islands in September, 1873, and . . . printed by the Treasury Department during my absence in Alaska. Owing to causes of which I have necessarily no knowledge, only 75 copies of this report were struck off; it was illustrated by 50 quarto plates photographed from my drawings and paintings" ("A Monograph of the Seal Islands of Alaska," U.S. Commission of Fish and Fisheries

Special Bulletin 176, 1882, p. 158). It is a beautiful book, with 227 unnumbered pages and 49—not 50—brown-tone lithographs. The title-page carries the date 1873, but the book was issued in 1874. Perhaps it was virtually suppressed because of statements of concern that "the Government may have men appointed to these Islands who are entirely incompetent or dishonest. . . . The frequent change of our public men in office who, like the Secretary of the Treasury, have the direction of a vast number of subordinates, will not guarantee . . . close scrutiny" (p. 43). In 1875 another book by Elliott, *A Report upon the Condition of Affairs in the Territory of Alaska,* was issued by the Government Printing Office. Although pages 63-164 closely resemble the 1874 publication, the statements quoted here do not appear. Elliott told his fur-seal story many times afterward, and the various versions were widely reprinted. There is apparently no bibliography of his publications, but they number at least twenty.

DAVID STARR JORDAN (ed.) *The Fur Seals and the Fur-Seal Islands of the North Pacific Ocean.* U.S. Treasury Department Document 2017, 4 parts. Washington, D.C. Government Printing Office, 1898-1899.

These volumes constitute the report of the Jordan commission, which came into being as a result of conditions in commercial sealing during the 1880s and 1890s. Seals were then being killed on the Pribilofs at a rate that surely exceeded the natural reproduction. In the 1880s at least 120,000 seals of Pribilof origin were being killed each year on land and sea, as compared to half that number today, and fewer and fewer seals were returning to the breeding grounds. In 1886, the United States Government seized three Canadian vessels and one American vessel engaged in pelagic sealing; this resulted in friction between Canadian and American diplomats. In late 1896, the United States accepted the proposal of Great Britain, acting for Canada, that the two countries independently study the biology of the Alaska seals and the effect of sealing on the brood stock, and the

BIBLIOGRAPHY

Jordan commission was appointed to represent the United States. It included David Starr Jordan, president of Leland Stanford Junior University and the greatest authority on ichthyology then living; Jefferson F. Moser, commanding the U.S. Fish Commission steamer *Albatross*; Leonhard Stejneger, curator of reptiles, U.S. National Museum; Frederic A. Lucas, curator of comparative anatomy, U.S. National Museum; and Charles Haskins Townsend, naturalist of the *Albatross*. George Archibald Clark, Jordan's secretary at Stanford, was appointed secretary of the commission, and Joseph Murray, then the government agent at St. Paul Island, was made a special assistant. The federal appropriation for the Jordan commission for two years was $5,000, plus $1,500 a year for its secretary. Its members visited the Pribilofs in 1896 and some returned in 1897. They mapped and photographed the rookeries, described the anatomy of the fur seal, studied its reproductive and food habits, and carried out many other biological investigations, all of which are covered in their report. Part 3 of the report contains translations of Steller and Veniaminov (see pages 193 and 194).

WILFRED H. OSGOOD, EDWARD A. PREBLE, and GEORGE H. PARKER. "The Fur Seals and Other Life of the Pribilof Islands, Alaska, in 1914," U.S. Bureau of Fisheries *Bulletin,* vol. 34 (1915), pp. 1-172.

A treaty to end pelagic sealing was finally signed by the United States, Japan, Russia, and Great Britain (representing Canada) on July 7, 1911; it remained in force until the outbreak of World War Two. About 1912, the seal population of the Pribilofs was at an all-time low of 200,000 animals. Then it slowly began to recover and by 1942 had leveled off at 1,700,000, representing an eightfold increase. In the spring of 1914, the Secretary of Commerce, who had been made responsible for the welfare of the seals, appointed three biologists to visit the Pribilofs. They were Wilfred H. Osgood, Field Museum of Natural History, Chicago; Edward A. Preble, Biological Survey, U.S.

Department of Agriculture; and George H. Parker, Harvard University. These biologists were chosen because they had no previous connection with the fur-seal problem and would therefore not be influenced by the controversies surrounding it. During their stay on the Pribilofs they carried on the kinds of studies that today would be called wildlife management research. They saw the need for obtaining key figures, such as the number of pups born each year, the number of harem bulls on duty and in reserve, and the number of bachelors returning each summer as indicated by the numbers in the sealing drives. They recognized that the proportion of harem bulls to reserve bulls could be a useful warning of overkilling, for if the reserve count should drop very low, it would mean that too few bachelors were being spared for breeding stock.

Their method of computing the size and composition of the herd was followed until the late 1940s.

F. H. C. Taylor, Motosaku Fujinaga, and Ford Wilke. *Distribution and Food Habits of the Fur Seals of the North Pacific Ocean.* Washington, D.C.: U.S. Fish and Wildlife Service, Government Printing Office, 1955.

This is the first account of international cooperation in fur-seal research. In 1952, biologists of Canada, Japan, and the United States collected on the open ocean over 3,000 fur seals. The Soviet Union had been invited to join the party but declined. The authors of the report, Fred Taylor (Canada), Motosaku Fujinaga (Japan), and Ford Wilke (United States), were biologists employed by the fishery agencies of their respective federal governments. Six research vessels hunted seals off the coast of northeastern Japan and two off the west coast of North America, from February to July, 1952. (The author of the present book was in charge of the American fleet.) The findings of the joint expedition included the following:

198

One-third of the seals wintering off Japan are of Pribilof origin, far from home.

Although the foods eaten in spring by seals of Asian and American waters are different, one-third of the volume of both consists of species of commercial value. The dollar values and food tastes of Japanese and Americans are also different. The lantern fishes and squids that contribute mainly to the diet of seals off Japan have little commercial value in America

Female Asian seals become sexually mature one year earlier than American seals; no one knows why.

Asian and American seals are indistinguishable unless they happen to be wearing tags.

The time of implantation, when the embryo begins to quicken, is in early November. This estimate was made possible by measuring over 400 fetuses.

The publication of the joint report hung fire for three years while statesmen of the three governments scrutinized it word by word for political implications. Its appearance in 1955 coincided with an expanding world-wide interest in resources of the sea, and the printing of 1000 copies was soon exhausted.

NORTH PACIFIC FUR SEAL COMMISSION. *Report on Investigations from 1958 to 1961* [Tokyo: Kenkyusha Co., 1964] Printed in Japanese, Russian, and English. The name of the printer and the date of publication are not shown on the English version.

On November 28, 1955, representatives of Canada, Japan, the Soviet Union, and the United States met to draft a fur-seal treaty to replace the one of 1912-1941. An Interim Convention was finally signed on February 9, 1957, and is still in effect. It provided for a standing committee of scientists whose duties would include research into the habits of seals on land and sea and also research into the economics of maximum sustainable yield. The first committee, which included biologists Gordon C. Pike (Canada), Fukuzo Nagasaki (Japan), Sergei Vasilievich Dorofeev (Soviet Union), and Ford Wilke (United States), after four years of research and international exchange of scientists, submitted this report. It is the best modern reference to statistics of the northern fur-seal herds. In addition to 21 pages of text, it contains 160 pages of tables and charts. It covers many aspects of fur-seal biology but is not a book to be read casually by laymen. The committee recommended a ban on pelagic sealing as a method of commercial harvesting, but year after year the Japanese continue to ask permission to kill fur seals from harpoon boats in coastal waters.

INDEX

INDEX

INDEX

About the Author

VICTOR B. SCHEFFER specialized in the study of marine mammals as a biologist with the United States Fish and Wildlife Service in Seattle, Washngton, from 1937 to 1969. During the summer of 1960, he was an observer for the Service on the Soviet fur seal island of Ostrov Tyuleniy. He visited Antarctica in 1964 as a member of the first inspection team sent by the United States Arms Control and Disarmament Agency under the terms of the Antarctic Treaty. Dr. Scheffer has lectured at the University of Washington on wildlife ecology and on the natural history of vertebrates. He received his Ph.D. from the University of Washington in 1936, is a member of Sigma Xi and Phi Beta Kappa, and received the United States Department of Interior's Distinguished Service Award in 1965. He is the author of *Seals, Sea Lions and Walruses,* published in 1958, and *The Year of the Whale,* for which he was awarded the Burroughs Medal in 1970 for the best book in the field of natural history. He and his wife live in Bellevue, Washington.

About the Illustrator

LEONARD EVERETT FISHER has illustrated over 100 books, including *The Year of the Whale.* He is also the author of a number of books. A native New Yorker, he studied at the Heckscher Foundation, the Art Students League, and the studio of Moses and Raphael Soyer. He was awarded the Pulitzer Art Prize in 1950.